A SPORTING ANGLER

A SPORTING ANGLER

Michael Prichard

Places, people and happenings that form the 'stuff of fishing'

COLLINS
WILLOW

To Leslie Moncrieff – in gratitude

First published 1987 by William Collins Sons & Co Ltd
London · Glasgow · Sydney · Auckland · Toronto · Johannesburg

Chapter Twenty one, Opportunist Angling, is based on an
article that was first published in *Angling News*.

The extract from *Sea Serpents, Sailors and Sceptics* by
Graham J. McEwan on page 122 is reproduced by kind
permission of Routledge & Kegan Paul.

Prichard, Michael
    A sporting angler.
    1. Fishing
    I. Title
    799.1'2'0924   SH439

ISBN 0 00 412138 4

Designed by Gail Engert
Text set in Linotron Palatino
by Rowland Phototypesetting Ltd, Bury St Edmunds, Suffolk

Printed and bound in Great Britain
by Robert Hartnoll (1985) Ltd, Bodmin

Frontispiece: **A Canadian small-mouth black bass.**

CONTENTS

Introduction

My sportfishing life has been one of deadlines to meet and articles to be written, with whatever illustration could be had in weather that was rarely ideal! In following the fish I have visited many countries, each with its own species to catch, methods to use and people to meet; and it has been the people who have given most to me! Fishermen are a friendly race, always competitive but never giving the feeling that you are 'on trial'! Without their help and guidance, life would have been extremely difficult.

Sportfishing for a living is a hazardous occupation. As a writer and illustrator one has to catch fish – or mix with anglers who do it for you. I always realized that it was asking a great deal to expect any fisherman to subjugate his natural desires and way of fishing to my wishes, to suggest that the magazine article or media programme should come first and that the real fishing must wait until the words were down on paper or the film safely spooled away in the can.

There are plenty of natural anglers who should be writing about their exploits, but who are content just to fish and to play down their successes rather than take up the pen! It is left to us, the sportfishing scribes, to chronicle the achievements of such men and, in doing so, make friendships that cross the barriers of time, nationality and politics.

I've had the pleasure of fishing with men who were millionaires, men who toiled for their daily bread in a humdrum employment, and primitive people who lacked any form of communication, other than a wise shake of the head or a fierce gesticulation that put me on the road to another fishing story with a successful ending. At no time did I ever get the feeling that my presence was an intrusion or that they, the local experts, were out to teach the 'city boy' a lesson. Fishing has no social barriers and one's reputation is simply measured by the way other anglers regard you as a sportsman and a companion with whom they would like to share another fishing day.

Many men have given me their wholehearted support and along the way taught me a great deal about the innermost things of the sport. Clive Gammon, that rumbustious Welshman, long since recognized by our American cousins who lured him across the Atlantic to the pages of *Sports Illustrated*, taught me mobility! Whether it was pike fishing at Bosherston or bass from the beaches of Kerry and West Wales, we always carried little on our backs – just enough simple tackle to let us search out the lies or follow the tide. Les Moncrieff was the technician, always providing yet another thought-out

A fisherman of Lagos, a small Algarve harbour on the southern coast
of Portugal, his open smile conveying, without language, all that a
specimen fish can mean to a man.

tackle that happened to be right or encouraging everybody in the party to
think like a fish! Sadly, during the preparation of this book, I learn of the death
of this dear friend. He came from a fabric and plastics industrial background
which gave him the profound engineering ability, with synthetic materials, to
develop new rods and other bits and pieces that improved our chances. Sea
angling has lost an innovator, though Leslie's 'layback' casting style will be
seen on European shores for a long time to come – serving as a reminder and
tribute to a great fisherman.

My understanding of the countryside came to me from my grandfather,
though it was Bernard Venables who showed me how to use that empathy to
make a living. I shall always be grateful for his freely given advice and for his
company on many trips to weird and wonderful places.

I have always believed that to be a successful angler one must attempt to be
a knowledgeable one! Knowing as much as possible about fish is important
but understanding their habitat even more so. One man, from the tiny hamlet
of Summercove in County Cork, instilled within me the urgent 'need to
know'. Alas, Professor Alexander Magri MacMahon is no longer with us, but
his memory lingers on my library shelves trapped within the pages of the
many books that he encouraged me to write.

When I retrace my steps to those places that gave me so much pleasure,
created stories and forced themselves on to these pages, I am sad. For all is not

as it was. In those few years the quality and quantity of sport has grievously declined.

Our seas are now arenas of confrontation, a commercial free-for-all despite agreements by politicians at their lush conferences, so graphically portrayed on our television screens. Although they mouth words of conservation, few nations really intend to preserve natural resources – except for themselves! When, despite conferences and agreements that some nations seem loth to ratify, the world's population of great whales seems destined for extinction, I ask myself – what chance do the fish have?

On land we have drainage schemes, often unnecessary, technical failures from scientists, whose qualifications might suggest a greater ability, and thoughtless proliferation of pollutants by all and sundry that spoil our freshwaters. There will always be somebody to persuade us inhabitants of the Northern Hemisphere that we need more land, that we should produce even more food, and that our national wealth depends on nuclear power stations or even bigger industrial plants. Is it really vital for us to be so wealthy?

I think I would prefer to have unpolluted forests where trees have healthy leaves. I am prepared to turn aside from the motorcar and walk into my wilderness – always provided that man has left a little! Ideally, there would be lakes and streams with clean, life-supporting water where I could fish. I have a terrible feeling that I may already have seen the best of fishing. I do hope that I am wrong.

The stories in this book result from fishing forays undertaken through the years 1960–1985 and I tell them in what is, roughly, a chronological order. To me, actual dates are less important than the sense of the passage of time – and the recounting of a good yarn.

The photographs in this book come from many parts of the world. Each carries a memory for me that is encapsulated within the particular environment. For sportfishing consists of places and happenings, with people tying each tiny event together so that they coagulate to form a fishing tale worthy of the telling. . . .

Michael Prichard
Emmen 1987

CHAPTER ONE

The Porbeagles of Clare

IRELAND

I firmly believe that Ireland, like no other place on Earth, possesses magical ingredients with the power to attract people back to her shores again and again. Sometimes stark in seascape, yet pleasantly soft inland, the wildness of the country is tempered by the sweetness of blended colours and the laughter of the people. I know Ireland well. I have tasted its moods and the vagaries of its weather; and it is to the roughest coastal limits that I am so often drawn. The cliffs of Clare, the yellow painted strands of Kerry and the hard shores of Mayo are to my liking.

The Atlantic Ocean, clean and ponderous, gives the West Coast an ecology hard to find anywhere else in the British Isles. Anglers prize the variety and quality of fishlife yet no crowds will ever be found on the open beaches or cluttering the tiny harbours that dot 'the West'. Fishermen arrive and are lost into the landscape. The only indication that other sportfishers are about is the occasional toot of a car horn, as they recognize your chosen calling from the laden roof-rack!

I call to mind one visit to the waters off the Cliffs of Moher, Ireland's highest sea cliffs that come rearing up from roiling seas off the Clare Coast.

The Inland Fisheries Trust had invited me, together with Leslie Moncrieff, then engaged in changing the British sea angling tackle scene with his designs for beachcasting rods and big-game tackle, to join in a semi-scientific appraisal of the porbeagle shark population that haunted the rocky reefs of this area. The task was to catch as many sharks as possible, using methods that would ensure their survival after returning them to the water. We would tag them so that they were immediately recognizable as the subject of a population survey, no matter where they swam to in the North Atlantic.

We travelled across Ireland to Lahinch to meet Kevin Linnane, then the Trust's sea angling officer. The town is both Kevin's birthplace and the site of one of Ireland's most famous golf links. Our interest, however, was in the tiny harbour at Liscannor, where the Trust's new research boat, *Finola*, lay canted to the rough stone wall. With any luck, the weather might give us a number of consecutive days on which to fish below the high buttresses that lead north from Hag's Head toward the indentation of Galway Bay.

Porbeagle are coldwater sharks that establish known territory, tending to choose rough and broken ground. The fish have a particular liking for pinnacle rocks and other forms of bulky, underwater reefs with an established population of pollack and other prey. Porbeagles will stay on a reef until lack of fodder fish forces them to move on to other hunting grounds. Kevin had researched the appearance, off the coast, of porbeagles by referring to the accurate records of Jack Shine, the first angler in Ireland to land porbeagles from the shore. More sound information came from the McArthy brothers, whose sharking exploits made many a headline in the angling press.

Some experiments had been done with trolled baits, not all of which had been successful. Nevertheless, sharks had shown enough interest to encourage further tests of this technique.

The first day's fishing started badly, when Kevin found that *Finola*'s cooling water wasn't circulating properly. After a cleaning job and filter changes, we left harbour to make our way out past Hag's Head into the rolling ocean swells. Mackerel were needed as hookbaits and as teasers, a baiting system that Les had seen used, to advantage, by American big-game fishers. A few minutes' feathering produced more than enough bait.*

BOX SWIVEL   STIFF WIRE MOUNT   TWIN MUSTAD 'SEAMASTER' HOOKS WELDED TOGETHER

SPLIT LINK

The porgie trolling rig: two 'Seamaster' hooks were welded together at right angles to ensure that we could strike immediately a fish attacked the trolled bait, this method gave us a perfect hookhold without harm to the fish.

We set up the baited rigs carefully. Mackerel, sliced open from the tail wrist to a point just behind the gillcase, had to be mounted on a stiff-wire, stainless steel rig that would let the secured bait swim in a natural fashion. We took out the backbones, sewing the double-hook rigs within the fish with thread. The lips of each bait were bound together with soft copper wire, so that the current of water, passing by the bait, would not enter the fish's mouth, creating pressure that might tear it from the baited mount.

Kevin had been experimenting with the dual engines to arrive at a suitable

---

* Before the massive predation by EEC commercial fishing boats, mackerel used to swarm off the Clare Coast in summer. The mackerel shoals have now been broken up into smaller groups and continued pressure, from East European fishing fleets, can only lead to the situation worsening!

trolling speed. With *Finola*'s motors just ticking over, we worked out the speed, through the water, of just over two knots. This meant that we had to add a 6-ounce weight to the trolled bait rig to keep it swimming about 12 inches below the surface. Les, anticipating that we might need something like the trolling leads, had bored a hole through a number of beachcasting weights before leaving his home in Kent. We set the weights to swim ahead of the baits, at a point where the stiff, baited mount met the flexible trace wire. We had decided upon fairly short wire traces, made in two sections, with quality swivels joining them in the middle and at each end. Each knot and ferruled connection had been thoroughly tested beforehand in England.

Choice of rod–reel combinations is always one of personal feeling! Les Moncrieff went for an IGFA outfit of 80-lb class, while I had chosen a lighter, 50-lb class set-up. My choice was simply based on the fact that, being nowhere close to Moncrieff in the physical strength stakes, I am prepared to take a little while longer to land a fish, with a lighter outfit that suits the pressure I can apply!

I confess a high regard for Penn reels and am fortunate in owning an International 30, which carries more than enough line for North Atlantic shark fishing. The reel, in fact, is among the most popular in the world's big-game fishing centres, for its smoothness of disc-applied drag and its satisfactory line capacity. I have kept the same sharking rod for many years. Made from an experimental blank, it has increased wraps of glass cloth under the left-hand position and though exactly balanced to IGFA 50-lb class, the tip is still responsive when used for a cod fishing session!

Recently I had the opportunity to inspect the Marquess of Sligo's rod, in Westport House, and came to the conclusion that his shark fishing exploits, in the early 1930s, must have been a backbreaking exercise. He and Dr O'Donnel Browne had caught giant porgies that stood as records for many years; and the head of the 365-lb porbeagle shark which Browne caught from a curragh rowed out from Keem Bay is still to be seen at the Achill Head Hotel. The Marquess's Hardy Saltwater No. 5 was a heavy rod, perhaps more suited to fishing for bluefin tunny or marlin. There can be no comparison between rods of that era, made from built cane, some with steel cores, and the light, responsive fibreglass and the latest carbonfibre weapons that we find nowadays among the serious sea angling fraternity.

Our first day's fishing out on an oily sea, broken only by the soft movement of long swells born far out in the middle of the Atlantic, saw us busy extending the teaser string. Kevin had wound a length of strong twine on to a drum with a suitable winding handle. We tied on a dozen mackerel, at one-yard intervals, and lowered the teaser shoal over the side to let it fall back about 50 yards behind the boat. The baited hooks, one to each of the two rods, were drifted back downtide to troll at about 40 yards behind *Finola*. Whether this method of attraction would work remained to be seen.

The first of our porbeagle shark is played away from the security of its home reef below Hag's Head. Les Moncrieff holds a steady pressure to turn the fish's initial run.

Big-game anglers of the tropical seas use teasers strung from outrigger poles so that the baits slap across the surface of the sea – a method, we thought, best suited for fishing species that hunt by sight. Our quarry, the porbeagle shark, hardly enjoys a reputation as a pelagic feeder except in places over nearly visible reefs, where it has been observed on the surface by lobster fishermen, potting on the same ground.

Out went the lines, straightening to the speed of the boat, as we settled *Finola* into a steady troll. Keeping close-in under the cliffs, we sought the exact location of the reef on the echo-sounder. A bulky pinnacle loomed high on the paper graph, with scattered black streak marks indicating the presence of small fish feeding high over the tips of the pinnacles. Pollack were one of the principal species that we expected to find, with wrasse further down the rock faces and some superb cod that we had been told were also resident.

We could see the teasers dancing from wave to wave, slapping the surface so realistically that lesser black-back gulls flew out from the cliffs to investigate. We made at least two passes along the cliff face before any action occurred. Then Kevin roared, 'Shark!' He has the eyes of a hawk, so was first to see the fin cutting through the water behind the teaser string. The fin swept off to one side and then veered sharply to bear in on the line of tethered mackerel. Frantic turning of the drum handle brought the teasers closer in to where the hookbaits swam, but the shark just sank from sight. We were distraught! Our first shark, seemingly following the baits but not sufficiently interested to strike at any of them. . . . After two or three repeats of the same tactics, we realized what was happening. The fish weren't going to be drawn away from their habitat, for the pinnacle rock territory contained enough resident food fish to make chasing a few mackerel unnecessary!

I know that this assumption smacks of anthropomorphism but, as the fishing progressed, shark after shark adopted the same flight behaviour! We tried, repeatedly, to follow exactly the same track across the reef, using both visual sightings on the cliffs and the echo sounder trace to establish our trolling pattern. Then we had the first real response from a fish; a flurry of spray, with frantic pulling on the teaser twine, indicated the arrival of a hungry shark. Winding in the twine, we found that two teaser mackerel had disappeared. Kevin put *Finola* into a wide circle to settle back on a reverse troll and we all had the satisfaction of seeing another shark cutting through the water, heading straight for the trolled baits. This fish swept in on the teasers sideways, missed them completely but then came upon a hookbait. Leslie's reel began to howl so he leapt across the deck to grab the rod from its holder. Kevin and I moved quickly to get the other rod bait and the teaser line in.

Les assured us that as soon as the shark had taken the bait, it turned and immediately sank down in the water, taking line against the pre-set drag and the travel of the boat as she lost forward speed; but it took no more line as we rolled, listlessly, on top of the low swells. The fish had apparently made for the seabed, at the base of the reef, and was content to lie there!

There aren't many fish that can resist the rod pressure that Moncrieff can apply. Slowly the shark began to move up through the depths as Les put a bend into his rod. Interestingly, it began to swim backwards and forwards across the face of the underwater buttresses – like a farm dog tethered on a long lead! Increased pressure brought the fish nearer to the boat. Occasionally visible, it began circling *Finola*, its fin cutting through the surface like a sail.

Leslie reckoned that we ought to play the sharks out as soon as their size and stubborn fight permitted, since to play any fish for a lengthy period, certainly until it was exhausted, wouldn't help its survival prospects at all. We agreed that fish had to be set free in a condition that guaranteed a perfect recovery from their exertions.

Ten minutes saw the first Clare porbeagle safely at the boat's side. Kevin had the tailing rope ready, spread around Leslie's feet, and as soon as the shark came within reaching distance I had the wire trace firmly grasped in my gloved hand. I tried to hold that fish as though it were a spaniel! Up went the tailing rope, over Leslie's head and the rod tip, to be shaken down the trace

Up comes the shark with the wire trace clear of its powerful pectoral fins. Hooked very lightly but secured by the tailing rope, this fish would not be harmed by its experience as hook removal was a simple operation.

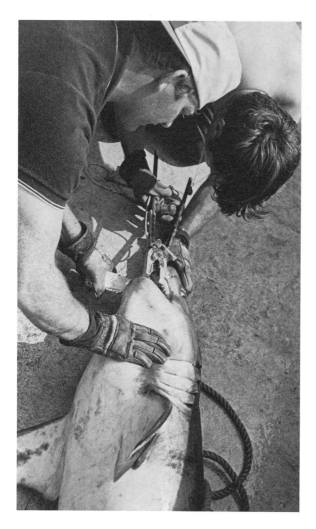

With both the tail and head of this shark restrained, the hook is removed from its jaw. A block of hardwood serves as a gag, holding the jaws apart.

A numbered, cattle ear tag applied to the trailing edge of the shark's dorsal fin will not impair the fish's swimming ability, but is easily detected upon recapture.

Kevin Linnane eases the shark back into the sea by slipping the tailing
rope noose. This shark was boated within a few hundred yards of the
Cliffs of Moher.

and around the shark's body. A quick pull from Kevin and the slipping noose
locked tight at the tail wrist. Then we all fell to hauling the shark, cautiously,
over the low gunwale. Great care is needed in boating any large shark;
considerable damage can be done to the internal organs, which are only really
protected by the body's cartilaginous framework when in a weightless
condition, were the fish to be suspended for any length of time.

Removal of the hook presented no problem. Trolling a bait ensures that the
shark is hooked, cleanly, in the mouth. As the fish strikes, it either stops in the
water or turns sharply, both actions stretch the line taut pulling the hook
home, setting it perfectly so that the angler hardly needs to sweep the rod

back to strike home the iron. We used Mustad Seamasters, a perfect big-fish hook that takes a good hold without working a large hole into the fish's flesh. Some finer metal hooks, though sharper, tend to wear a hole very quickly. Over the years, Les and I have settled for the undoubted qualities of the Seamaster for all our game fishing in the sea.

The Inland Fisheries Trust had provided us with cattle ear tags and pliers to fix them in the trailing edge of the fish's dorsal fin, easily visible, in the future, to sportfishermen and commercial operators alike. Kevin squeezed the two halves of the plastic tag home, while we logged the fish's size, sex and tag number. Then we all three lifted the fish back across the gunwale. Slipping the shark back into its own environment gave us enormous satisfaction. Having subjected it to the minimum of stress, we hoped it would live and possibly provide the Trust with useful information if it was recaptured.

During our week's stay we had 28 porbeagle sharks and a couple of blues. All, with the exception of one fish destined for dissection, went back into the sea within a minute or so, a simple flick of the tail driving them deep toward the seabed. It took us a little longer to recover from our own exertions.

We learned later that the Trust had some returned tags from our fish. One came from Cape Finisterre and the other from somewhere off the Azores. Both were taken by commercial fishing boatmen who returned the tags to Dublin, but gave no indication of the condition of the migratory fish when recaptured on their long-lines. Since that time, other sharks have been caught and marked, by more sophisticated methods. One can only hope that a fair number of these fish avoided ending up on the deck of a commercial fishing boat, and made a successful return journey to the pinnacle reef below the Cliffs of Moher.

CHAPTER TWO

The Prolific Waters of Achill

IRELAND

More than twenty years ago, irresistibly impelled to explore the sportfishing of deepsea marks off the rugged west coast of Ireland, I got my first glimpse of the stark landscape of Achill. I paid small attention then to the towering mountain that cast its shadow across the deserted village and wet, upland bog. Only later did I appreciate the nature of the island, a place of strangers, to which men and women came for a few weeks each year to freshen their minds, enjoy the ample solitude, and yet meet daily in the tiny pubs to compare their reactions to the sight and sounds of this remote spot.

Achill can't really be called an island nowadays; for years it has been connected to the mainland of County Mayo by a bridge at The Sound. Yet, there still remains the sense of being in a land apart. The inhabitants, Celtic and withdrawn, have the ruddy complexion and bent shoulders that tell of year-round toil in an unfriendly environment which treats animals and humans alike. Achill's land mass juts out into the North Atlantic, breaking the full force of weather born far out in mid-ocean. Because of its location and the happy coincidence that the North Atlantic Drift curls around its shores, Achill enjoys quality sea fishing. Many of the species present are resident, yet there is an annual migration of fish, large and small, into the surrounding seas that has given the island an unrivalled reputation among the sea fishermen of Europe.

One day, as I was leaning against the tiny harbour wall at Purteen, I met Percy Huet, the kind of philanthropist who can be found in many isolated places around the world; a man, then elderly, eager to share his love of the island life and his knowledge of the fishing with strangers. Percy also encouraged the local people to improve their lot by taking visiting anglers out to fish in the waters of the bay. For this purpose he had bought two boats: *Grainne*, a 30-foot traditional lobster craft with a powerful diesel engine, and a 21-foot carvel hull, powered by an outboard, known simply as *Twenty-One*! His modest efforts to promote the fortunes of his beloved Achill were shared by two other Irishmen, policeman Charlie Walsh and commercial skipper Jim

Open quarter-deckers were our boats. Seaworthy, double-ended craft made to match all that the Atlantic could throw at them. The carvel hulls are ideal for the scend of the ocean.

Men of Achill, Percy Huet (left) and Charlie Walsh were the driving force behind sportfishing from the island. Percy has made certain of his dinner – a plump autumn cod.

O'Gorman, both of them avid anglers, yet neither of them local to the island.

These gentlemen were determined that my first trip to sea in Achill should be a baptism of fire! My earlier sea angling exploits failed to impress them – compared to the conditions that Achill could throw at a man. Swells that grew in mid-Atlantic could roll in as high as a house; a surging power that spent its energy on the giant sea cliffs and dangerous, half-hidden reefs, and had taken many a life.

We took *Grainne* north-west from the shelter of Purteen, past a rocky coastline, almost lunar in construction. Weaving through the harbour entrance and pushing inside the grass-topped isle of Inishgalloon, we made for a reef that showed, sporadically, above the swells. The Dysaghy Rocks, as they are called, exhibit a peculiar phenomenon. Under pressure of an uneven

swell, a tremendous water spout rises between the two masses of rock that form the underwater reef. The sea, around the reef, is troubled with irregular currents that sweep in to form eddies and sudden surges that are a hazard to any boat. Percy had given the skippering of *Grainne* to a young man, Pat Kane. Together with old James Gavin, a man of the sea from Keel village, Pat was bent on proving the fish-holding capabilities of this mark.

Setting a boat's drift, so that it rides safely past but alongside any reef demands a sure knowledge of the current's direction and strength at any state of tide. Pat looked for a nod from James as indication that the boat was correctly headed, but never switched the engine off while on the drift. Although many sea anglers would regard that as a noise factor liable to spoil the fishing, it was comforting in these dangerous waters to know that the skipper could get an immediate response if a rogue swell threw us at the hazardous reef!

Most sea fishers, in my experience, are content to fish the bottom, the methods and tackle being directly related to fish that feed, exclusively, at the seabed. There, on the Dysaghy Rocks, was a situation that needed a total alteration of approach. The inhabitants of the reef were mid-water feeders, species that live in the thousands of crevices and among the weeds that abound below the water's surface. As we settled to the beginning of the drift, James explained, in his soft lilting manner, the fishing ways of his forbears, telling of men who had braved the wild ocean to fish handlines from traditional curraghs, boats made from tarred canvas skins laid over a framework of wooden laths, affording scant safety but a manoeuvrability unheard of in modern craft! He promised pollack and sea bream, to be fished for with slivers of fresh mackerel, which first had to be caught.

Out went the feathers into the creaming spindrift, downtide of the reef. In minutes we had hundreds of thrashing baitfish aboard. Some were for our hookbait but many were put aside for the old folk of the village, who counted on the 'odd bit of fish' to supplement their diet! Then we set to filleting the mackerel, cutting each individual lash into narrow slivers.

Back in those days sea angling tackle was, to say the least, a trifle ham-fisted

A dangerous yet most prolific mark, the Dysaghy Rocks in the middle of Achill Bay. In the background are The Bills, another outstanding area for specimen fish.

and over-strong. Somewhere I had acquired a Hardy saltwater spinning rod 8 foot in length, which I intended pressing into service. Balanced to a multiplying reel, loaded with 10-lb nylon, I felt more than equipped for the forthcoming drifts. Although my companions were less fortunate, having only standard boat rods and the sea angler's staple line, 30-lb nylon, we all turned to fishing sink and draw along the face of the reef. Sport hit us immediately as fish grabbed at the baits in mid-water. Rods thumped over in graceful curves, a sure indication that fast-moving pollack were down below and eager to feed.

The pollack we boated appeared close to the weight set by the Inland Fisheries Trust as specimen size. Then some of us had delicate, sucking bites as we lowered our baited rigs. 'Bream', whispered James, upturned pipe clenched between his teeth, and he glanced around at his marks on the shore and *Grainne*'s distance from the main bulk of the reef. Repeated bites and swift striking brought no contact with the fish, and it dawned on me that we had a simple problem – known at that time as the 6/o syndrome! Most sea anglers would automatically tie on a big 6/o hook, since there seemed to be many more large fish for the taking than nowadays! Dropping down in size to 1/os immediately gave yanking bites that slammed the rod tips over the gunwales. My own disappeared below the waterline as soon as a fish took the bait, and

Something to make a sea angler's heart race: mackerel spattering the surface as they harry a brit shoal. Often larger fish can be detected as they drive upward to feed on the preoccupied mackerel.

even the lads armed with conventional boat rods were momentarily convinced that the bites must be from huge pollack!

Then the first fish came up to the surface. It was a red bream, a handsome fellow, brilliantly coloured in hard gold and red scaling. It weighed over 4-lbs, which made it an automatic qualifier for a specimen fish award. But there were more to come as one after the other we all hooked and fought the flashing slab-sided 'darlings' into the side of the boat. The bream were larger than any we had seen in years of sea fishing. Gradually, as the reef fell away behind us, the bites tailed off to nothing, so Pat nudged the Lister into gear and we motored quietly uptide to begin another drift.

A nod from James and the gear lever was slipped into neutral. Our position was slightly off on a different track to take account of the subtle change in tide direction. Fishing started much as before, with almost instant response from the pollack as the baits reached mid-water. Since the size of the fish did not vary much, I chatted with Pat about the pollack marks that he had pinpointed in his time as an Achill boatman. He mentioned, as everyday experience was beginning to prove, that there were so many areas of rock and foul ground in Achill Bay that fish, of widely differing dimensions, tended to choose a location relative to their size. He suggested proving this by moving off to a mark, just outside Purteen, behind the rocky island of Inishgalloon, where the seabed was made up of huge slabs of rock lying in terraced shelves!

After consultation and a few muttered oaths from the lads who had yet to catch one of the larger bream, we headed south for the new ground. Unfortunately, the new drift started to drag the weights into the slabs, rather than across the flat shelves, bringing a rash of line breakages. One cheerful man from Kent, using a really massive rod and braided line as thick as your finger, got fast in the bottom and couldn't break out. In fact, he held the boat for a few moments, and then, with a staccato crackling sound, three rings were ripped away from their whipping to bunch up at the rod tip. Laughter pealed on the breeze as he admitted that his gear was probably more suited to skate fishing than pollack over the reefs. After remaking terminal rigs, we found that the pollack were there on the flat rocks. They were bigger and harder to fight to the top, although there was a lot less water under the keel than we had fished on the Dysaghys.

Looking at the fish coming inboard, we decided to take in only those that could be about specimen weight. The condition of these pollack, with sleek dark green backs, shading to a brilliant creamy-bronze on the bellies, was new to most of us, for they were hard as a board and full of fight. My rod was put to the test and subjected to a fighting curve never intended by the makers. I decided, there and then, to spend some time building a slightly stronger rod with faster taper based on the same principle of light tackle fishing. The rod, in fact, was made during that winter and christened 'The Achill Sportsman'. It went to the same marks in the following year . . . but that is another tale!

Evening in Achill

'Après fishing hours' on Achill tended to follow a familiar routine. At dinner in the Amethyst Hotel we were stimulated to the heights of gluttony by the fair ministrations of Thea Boyd who fervently believed in feeding fishermen well. Then, although the guests were hardly able to rise from the refectory table, somebody would casually mention the 'Annexe'. This pub, the over-the-road part of the hotel – was owned and managed in a way that can only be described as anachronistic by the late Captain Robert Boyd, one-time member of the Irish Army and husband of our hostess. Robert believed in all things Irish, which meant adhering to the rules of a traditional hostelry of 'the Wesht'! Ceiling beams that fractured the skulls of the unwary had been built in strategic positions; an open fire had a permanently blazing bank of turf climbing up the chimney; and the rough-hewn tables bore witness to count-less spillages from pints of porter, long since emptied down throats that between sips roared out refrains in praise of the Irish landscape or the Irish mother.

Bar talk never wandered far from the sea and its fish. Nightly, a band of interesting souls would be drawn by the light streaming from the windows. One picture postcard salesman from Dublin, full of travellers' tales and never without two charming girls on his arms, would gleefully recount the day's happenings on his round of the farmhouses and tiny hotels that took their guests from England and farther afield. Each evening he would be begged to repeat the tale of the Old Country Wife who found herself in court after some ticklish business. 'Your Honour, me Lord, Sir, she said', were the opening lines of a story too risque to reproduce in these pages, but guaranteed to bring tears to the eyes of the company as they willed the narrator to the punchline!

We became used to the soft, cosy atmosphere so different from the harsh life that existed beyond the firelight of the bar. Closing time, if it ever came, was a moment eagerly awaited. The varied reasons, calculated to weaken the resolve of our pretty barmaid, for pouring another pint of Guinness were hilarious. Twinkling eyes in weatherbeaten faces, searched the lass for a sign that she might just 'bend to the wind' and splash the dark brown liquid, that binds Ireland together, into another glass.

Charlie Walsh, the local Garda, had a delightful way of maintaining discipline among the unruly. During the course of the evening Charlie would appear in a battered *bainin* sweater, with an equally well-used knitted bobble cap. This 'uniform' and the fact that he would allow us to buy him pints, signified that all was well with the company and the evening, setting a seal of approval on our behaviour. Amid the drinking and angling chatter we never did notice Charlie slip away until he came back through the Annexe door dressed somewhat differently, the rough, knitted woollens having been exchanged for an old sports jacket, crowned by a porkpie hat. This was the semi-official policeman's garb intended to establish to one and all that Charlie was firmly in control!

The evening would get wilder, the singing higher pitched, while the Paddy bottles and pints would flash across the bar in quick monetary exchange. We all knew that the hour was late, with only a few hours to snatch some sleep before the call to a massive breakfast followed by another day on the water. But men, especially when in Ireland, never learn! Finally the late edition was delivered. Charlie Walsh would stride through the door, his great bulk now clothed in the full regalia of the Garda Siochaina. It was clearly get out – or suffer the consequences. I believe that one or two hard cases spent a night or so at the barracks before they began to read Charlie's appearances correctly.

With Mangan at Achill Head

One bright Achill day, with only a riffle of wind to bend the clouds, Percy stated emphatically, 'This is a day for The Head!' Mine wasn't feeling too good after the previous night's entertainment, but Percy was referring to the long peninsula of cliffs that extend seawards beyond Moyteoge Point. Apparently there were days when the weather was fit for a boat to fish the rough ground at The Head, although many more when only a fool would attempt it! With Pat Kane at the tiller and the anglers aboard, we awaited the arrival of Percy's Volkswagen truck at the harbour. The word was that he would be slightly delayed as he had to take one of our skippers, Jim O'Gorman, to the doctor. It was many years before I learned that each morning's small delay was the result of a 'one drink' visit to the Annexe!

When they finally arrived, Percy and Jim O'Gorman had a companion. A big, broad-shouldered, elderly man with a wide smile and a delightful use of few words. Big Tony Mangan was to be our guide to the fishing of the Achill Head, our echo sounder, if you like, for it was acknowledged that his feel for the ground was unsurpassed. Off we went as he settled himself on the stern thwart, alongside young Pat Kane, explaining the marks, pointing out reference details ashore while talking the boat through its passage along the coast.

It was to be bottom fishing and big fish could be expected. Mangan nearly threw a fit when he saw our light tackle, but I doubt he realized the value of a rod as a spring inserted between the fighting fish and the angler. Anyway, we started a drift close to a diabolical chunk of rock that reared skywards momentarily as each swell swept past leaving the trough to expose what the sea had in store for the unwary boatman.

Mackerel was the bait. We hadn't bothered to feather on the way out as we had some aboard and Pat said that there would be a thick shoal around The Head. He was right. The leaping, gleaming speedsters started grabbing our whole lashes intended for the bottom-feeding fish. I felt my 6-ounce lead

Big Tony Mangan . . . and a tub gurnard from The Head. The mark could always be relied upon to produce several very large tub gurnards, along with a smattering of the red species.

Perfect fishing grounds have their hazards; this almost submerged reef
marks the start of our drift at Achill Head. Wherever the reefs showed
– so did the fish, in abundance.

bouncing on the backs of mackerel as they swirled below *Grainne*. Looking up,
we found that Jim O'Gorman had nudged his *St. Patrick* into a parallel drift.

The first fish came to Dennis Burgess, an old friend of mine who has the
capacity to land huge fish and sink a few pints in the telling of how he does it!
Dennis shouted that the fish had grabbed his bait and moved away a bit; then
everything had gone solid. Only occasional movements, described by Dennis
as head-shaking, gave a clue to the species. Most of us had had enough
experience, in distant waters, to recognize the opening gambit from a large
cod. Minutes later, for it was a full 30 fathoms to the bottom, the creamy,
yellow-marbled belly of a 20-lb cod broke the surface – not a bad start to an
Achill day!

We were all somewhat surprised to find ourselves taking a different quality
species on each drop down. The catch consisted predominantly of cod,
pollack, ling, coalfish, cuckoo wrasse and a number of huge bull huss, while

A picture from the scrapbook: my first Achill cod, a fish of 20 lbs that came from the foul ground beneath the towering cliffs marking the edge of Ireland.

tope and spurdogs arrived when the drift took *Grainne* away from the reef. Most of us changed to a single hook on our flowing traces as it became evident that using two hooks meant two fish hooked, one or both of which would tear themselves from the rig on the way to the surface. Two fish pulling against each other, combined with the vertical pressure exerted by the angler, often causes the loss of everything. Results exceeded all expectations and we needed no further proof from our hosts that this was indeed 'Big Fish Country'.

Competition Day

When sea fishing is near perfect, it is easy to become blasé. To enliven one of our trips to Achill, our hosts suggested a competition day with a difference. Instead of a match which involved catching more weight than one's companions, they had devised a contest based on bringing home the maximum number of species. What an innovative day that turned out to be!

Our chosen sport is not one naturally geared towards species selectivity. So many marine species live in the same habitat, feeding with similar motivation, that an angler cannot separate them merely by selective tackle techniques or baits. Early morning, therefore, saw us all at Purteen discussing, with our respective skippers, tactics most likely to win the day.

Pat Kane was again skippering my boat and as the youngest of Achill's skippers had the most difficult task in deciding where to go. He wasn't above taking advice from his anglers for, although he knew well where to fish for the popular species, he only had a sketchy knowledge of the smaller fish that might swing the competition in *Grainne*'s favour.

We spent little time hanging around at the harbourside. Everybody was aboard within minutes and Percy roared us off with a demand for turbot, a fish that didn't often grace the Achill kitchens. The locals watching onshore could only wonder at the apparent madness of the English anglers as all three boats tore around the bay, from mark to mark. No sooner were we anchored than the engine was started, the anchor raised and off would go the boat to what was apparently a similar patch of grey water!

We decided to give everyone a chance to catch at least one of each species offered by the successive patches of seabed. With four anglers in the boat, we agreed to fish for five minutes after the third angler got his chosen fish, and then to go looking for a different species. Inevitably we couldn't all fill the quota, no matter how hard we fished. Good humour prevailed, however, and after six hours serious angling in a rising wind and swell, we came up with a

Twenty-seven species caught during a competition day must be some sort of record. The smallest – a greater sandeel from Keem Bay; the largest a porbeagle that cruised off Moyteoge Pt.

tally of nineteen species, confident of being among the prizes – beautiful hand-made pottery and crockery from the monastery at Pontoon. So we were astonished to see no less than twenty-seven species laid out on the harbour-side at our landing point. It was a fantastic achievement, by any standard, for the fishers who went to sea with Jim O'Gorman. They had practically everything that Achill Bay could offer in rod and line fish, the lowliest a greater sandeel, the largest a porbeagle shark.

Our species day had been a great success, the anglers displaying ingenuity in tackle and bait presentation, and the three skippers justifying their knowledge of the chosen sea area. I'm not sure that my nerves would stand a repetition of the exercise but, deep down, I have a yearning to get the same lads to Mayo where we might just crack it once more!

Keem Bay and basking sharks

There was a time, not so long ago, when the fishermen of Achill augmented their hard-won incomes by netting and harpooning basking sharks. It is a form of fishery that has been practised, in a few discrete islands around Ireland and Scotland, for a very long time. Basking sharks have enormous livers which, rendered down in a heated vat, provide one of the finest machine, medicinal and lamp oils known to man. The problem faced by the fishermen has always been where to dispose of the carcasses. Considering that a fair sized basker can weigh two tons, we get an idea of the amount of flesh to be rid of!

The Achill men solved their annual dilemma by towing the strongly-smelling carcasses away from the harbour and the tourists to Keem Bay where, at Moyteoge Point, they were sunk to the seabed. Unwittingly, the commercial fishermen were providing sea anglers with a new fishing location. A multitude of crabs and other crustaceans fed upon the disintegrating carcasses. Shoals of sandeels came to populate the sandy seabed at the outer extremity of the bay. Within months the bottom was alive with flatfish, mostly dabs, but including a few 'chicken' turbot: fish of 3–4 lbs that found the fodder fish species to their liking.

We happened on this larder of 'flats' quite by chance. I went down to Keem Bay with Dora and Leslie Moncrieff on a shorefishing foray. We had intended duplicating the trek made by Lady Sligo when she went porbeagle spotting for her husband from the cliffs at Moyteoge Point. Discretion led us to take up casting out from the firm sand of the tiny, golden strand that rings the inner crescent of the bay instead of risking a doubtful perch on the wet grass of the sloping cliffs.

We had dug some fresh lugworm on the strand, below the Burvie, at Keel. So, baiting up legered traces, both Les and I cast toward the floating boxes in which the lobstermen keep their catch fresh. Almost at once we had small,

tweaking pulls to the baits that neither of us could strike or make contact with. Missing bite after bite can be frustrating, to say the least, so off I went to cool my temper with a stroll at the water's edge.

On the wet sand, at the point where each successive wave spills its foam, I saw a momentary flash of silver. Scooping away the sand, I found the smallest of sandeels. Gathering quite a few very easily, I tipped them into the bait bucket and trudged back along the sand. The sneaky bites had continued and Leslie was getting madder by the minute! His guess was for rough hounds that were satiated with feeding on the putrefying shark carcasses. In optimistic mood, we both threaded on a tiny eel to join the lugworm bait.

What a pleasant surprise for Moncrieff; a 'chicken' turbot that grabbed the first of our tiny sandeel baits. This was one occasion when lugworms did not succeed!

With the next bite, Leslie's rod walloped over and began bouncing to the strong pull of a hooked fish. While reeling in, he shouted along the strand that he had at last hooked a dog! There isn't a lot of fight from a chicken turbot, so Les could be forgiven for denigrating his fish. As soon as the turbot appeared I made a rush to attend my own rod, which was in the rest 'fishing for itself'. Soon I also had a turbot and from there on it was one after the other. We finished up with enough fish to feed the entire guest-list at the Amethyst Hotel. Within the catch there were a couple of plump dabs, thick and well-fleshed from feeding on whatever the bay's sharks had drawn. It seemed, on reflection, that the flatfish were not really interested in serious feeding as there was so much natural food about. Only when we baited our hooks with the tiny, silver sandeels had they become tempted.

Alas, recent trips to Keem Bay have not come up to expectations. Like most of the British Isles coastline, Mayo's littoral waters are subjected to massive predation by commercial fishing. Offshore sandbanks, marked on fishing charts of old-timers of forty years ago or more, seem barren of turbot that were once a prolific species. More optimistically, however, trawling has yet to reduce the amount of fish that haunt the foul ground of the Bay and around The Bills, rocks that rise 124 feet from the waves south-west of Keel.

The surfers

It was in this same area that I came across an instance of animal behaviour with almost a human pattern to it. About eight years ago I was driving south on yet another fishing visit to Ireland with Mike Shepley, from the tiny hamlet

A lone porpoise hurls its body clear of curling breakers below the Cliffs of Minaun, Achill Bay. No doubt it was heading seaward to seek a huge breaker – and another exhilarating ride!

of Dooagh, toward Keel village on Achill Island. It was a stormy day with a brisk onshore, westerly wind that caused long lines of breakers to form at least a quarter of a mile offshore. From a distance of a mile I saw what I at first assumed to be surfers on their boards, skimming in to the sand. Driving further into the village the thought seemed unrealistic; after all it was late autumn, the weather was cold and Achill is not exactly known as a haven for surfplankers!

There was nothing for it but to drive out, across the links toward Keel Strand, to get close to the sea. The 'surfers' were still at their sport, flashing in on the creaming water. Out came the binoculars for a closer look. Imagine our surprise when it became apparent that the 'surfers', under the shadow of the Cliffs of Minaun, had fins!

The sporting creatures were porpoises, playing like children in the crests of the rolling breakers. Just like their human counterparts, they rode in the crests and then swam back out to sea to begin the play once more. I had never witnessed or heard of this behaviour before. Luckily Mike and other companions were there to watch the activity, over a period of more than half an hour, before the animals sped off in the direction of Clare Island. Mike insisted that the animals deliberately waited to catch the big wave, idling between the smaller swells until a fancied one arrived. Then they rode the creaming crest into the shore.

Photography, under prevailing weather and distance conditions, prevented quality pictures; but I have just one, massively enlarged, shot that shows a porpoise leaping as a line of surf swirls beneath its body!

CHAPTER THREE

Sesimbra and Swordfish

PORTUGAL

Bernard Venables looked up from his daily pile of letters and asked casually, 'Is your passport in date?' A simple question in the 'Creel' office that started us both on a journey into the world of big-game fishing.

News had filtered through the angling grapevine that European fishers had at last cracked the monopoly of a huge oceanic species previously confined to American and other exotic fishing venues. A tiny holiday resort south of Lisbon had leapt into the frame with catches of broadbill swordfish that ranked with anything taken on the far side of the world.

We were headed for Sesimbra to join a party of Portuguese anglers who were pioneering a new system for catching the broadbill. Not for them the trolling of baits or hours spent quartering the sea looking for the sign of a fin that denoted a fish basking at the surface in the heat of summer! This was long-line country where scores of tiny aiolas, stout rowing boats, were daily taken out over the 90-fathom deep water to lay hundreds of metres of nylon longline for the Ray's bream that formed the best part of their deepwater catch.

Commercial fishermen who had lost an enormous quantity of fish, torn from the lines, had initially blamed the Atlantic shark population. One day, however, there came a sharp pull on the lines and a fish so wrapped up in nylon that it was unable to get free was hauled to the surface. The predator proved to be a broadbill swordfish. Empty hooks on the lifted lines showed that it had been feeding at the depth setting associated with Ray's bream.

Sportfishers, quickly alerted to the presence of the billfish, started by chartering small commercial boats to tow a number of aiolas out to the fishing grounds. In the early 1950s they provided themselves with the purpose-built, big-game boat *Pioneiro*, but this was subsequently converted into a ferry boat after the anglers decided that it was more convenient and rewarding to go on fishing from the smaller, rowing craft.

A dinghy was ideal, in any event, for getting the hookbait in among the long-lining commercial boats and down to where the big fish were! Once in

Bernard Venables, who launched 'Angling Times' and 'Creel', has
spent his life fishing, writing and painting pictures of his creatures and
countryside. Together we fished in many parts of the world.

position, a bream provided by the lining skipper was attached to a big hook
and lowered to approximately where the fish shoals and likely predators were
thought to be.

Then it became a waiting game. Strikes weren't made everyday; sometimes
the angler had to wait weeks for a broadbill to attack the hookbait. Probably
the close proximity of hundreds of hooked fish alerted any broadbill inspecting the noise and vibration that are part and parcel of the long-lining
underwater disturbance. It took several seasons of research before a productive pattern of sportfishing emerged.

A live hookbait had to be mounted on a 14/0–16/0 hook, with the iron taken
through the back of the fish just below the dorsal fin. Time had shown that
this neither killed nor impaired the mobility of the bait. Ray's bream can
evidently be hauled up by the liner, lowered back to 90 fathoms to fish and
then hauled up again for inspection, without apparent undesirable pressure
effect.

Each dinghy was slowly rowed around the lining activity, never too close to
tangle the working lines, but always stemming whatever tide there was. A
strike, when it came, was registered as a sharp slap on the line. The angler
immediately pulled off free line and 'threw it to the fish', somewhat akin to
the reaction of a salmon fly angler.

During my first day's fishing, I saw three strikes close to my camera
position on the large boat. One resulted in a hooked fish and, thanks to the
long duration of the fight, I was able to follow everything that happened.

The angler reacted to the slap from the swordfish by letting out a lot of line, 50 feet or so. As he and his boatman engaged in a shouting match, the boatman leaned over his shoulder, as though to grab the line or slam the reel into gear! The man with the rod replied with what was presumably the Portuguese version of two stiff fingers; although his boatman's screams must have had some effect for the rod was thrown back to set the hook. For a moment nothing happened and I thought that here was another one to get away!

Then the rod began to bend over, not fast, yet with power and certainty. I imagine that the fisherman had already adjusted an amount of drag of the 16/0 reel he was using, for the rod tip kept nodding, which is a sure sign that the clutch is slipping, perhaps not too evenly, definitely giving line. Since the aiola was also moving, stern first, the boatman gave his oars an occasional sweep to keep its axis in a direct line to the fish. The boat moved away quite quickly and I lost perfect vision until Francisco, skipper of the large launch, started his engines and began following at a discreet distance.

At first the fisher made no attempt to recover line, but just sat bolt upright on the gimballed seat, his gloved left hand on the drum of the reel. The dinghy continued to move deliberately through the water in a wide circle but

With a swirl the fish breaks the surface after a prolonged fight. This broadbill towed the aiola for what seemed like hours before arriving at the gaff.

gradually slowed – a clear sign that its weight was affecting the broadbill's swimming ability. I had taken a close look, earlier, on the parent boat, at the six angler's reels, which were filled with 130-lb American, braided Dacron line, surely strong enough to allow the towing behaviour without fear of a breakage.

That broadbill towed for twenty-five minutes before there was any serious reaction, other than vocal, from the angler! What happened next astonished me! The angler started to recover line without making any attempt to pump the rod. He simply grabbed the line below the butt ring with his gloved hand, pulled like blazes and wound on the recovered line. He probably reckoned that he was recovering line by lifting the fish, but I believe the reality was quite different!

As he pulled line back, the boat moved toward the fish, thus effectively shortening the amount of line out. Yet it seemed doubtful that his action was helping to kill the swordfish, which merely went on towing the boat. After something close to an hour and a half, he was still pulling the line back and the dinghy was still moving about. Obviously the fish was being worn down by its own exertions and it was not until the last ten minutes of the fight that the angler's efforts were appreciably and directly transmitted to the fish.

When we eventually got a glimpse of the fish, it looked well and truly exhausted. While the angler finally made an attempt to reel in the last of the line above the trace, the boatman gently rowed the boat toward the broadbill, which now lay quietly on the surface. I saw the boatman gaff the fish and then, seconds later, the angler leaned over the gunwale of the dinghy and came up with the hook in his hand. He turned to us, jubilantly waved the hook in the air and paid no attention to the poor lad holding the gaff. I saw no sign of an attempt to rope the tail as the fish lay alongside the aiola, but suddenly sounds of a fierce quarrel echoed across the dividing water! Apparently the broadbill had decided to roll off the gaff!

The boatman made frantic attempts to gaff it again, not aided at all by the angler who spent his time either holding his head in his hands or screaming at the top of his voice. The fish quietly slipped away below the waves. The arm waving and the tears lasted for a full ten minutes.

The next day's fishing started badly. There was an embarrassed silence between crew and anglers as *Pioneiro* carried us out to the commercial fishing area. The unlucky protagonist of the previous day's fiasco hid himself forward, only emerging when we stopped to transfer the rods to the aiolas. As we settled to our long wait for action, the skipper explained that the rod and line handling methods were devised by a man from Lisbon who had 'found' and pioneered fishing for broadbill off Cape Espichel.

Later in the week I had the pleasure of seeing a solid strike become a hooked and boated fish. On this occasion the fish fought for a much shorter time, although the rod handling method was identical to that used a few days before. Again we saw nothing of the broadbill during the fight for, as is customary with the species, it took the bait deep and stayed down in the depths until almost defeated. This time the man in the fighting chair made no mistakes with the beaten fish, tailing it and securing it to the aiola before retrieving the hook!

Francisco and I had a heart-stopping moment in the early afternoon. One of the rods had decided to come on to the larger boat to take his lunch. Placing his rod in an inclined holder, he left the bait dangling somewhere below the keel of *Pioneiro*. Our eating activities were shattered by the scream of the reel and we all watched in amazement as yards of line disappeared, at a hell of a speed, off the drum. The line straightened behind the boat and, some ten seconds or so later, a broadbill hurled itself into the air about 100 yards behind the boat. We could see the bait clearly, held across the bill of the fish, which hit the water and came out again, this time swinging its head sharply and flinging the bait to the side. Then, with a tremendous flurry of spray, the fish hit the water's surface and was gone. The entire action took no more than ten or twelve seconds, though the argument and the cursing aboard our boat lasted a great deal longer!

Clearly this was a fish that had been cruising just below the surface, perhaps sunning itself, without any fear of the boat activity. It may well have followed a string of hooked bream up from the depths, before attacking within a few yards of us! At one time, so I was told, there was a famous family of commercial fishermen from Sesimbra who specialized in harpooning swordfish as they lay sunning themselves at the surface. The harpooner would stand at the end of an extended catwalk, way ahead of the bulk of the boat. As soon as a fish was sighted, the engine revs were cut and the boat glided silently toward it. For some reason, whenever an angler offered a bait to a fish lying at peace on the surface, it was refused! So the harpoon was the only solution.

Swordfishing proved a fascinating experience for me. Here was one of the world's largest gamefish which repeatedly foiled the catching tactics of experienced anglers. Despite the enormous number of daily strikes, during the peak season, very few fish were actually boated. It wasn't the bulk of the fish or its power that beat the angler. I truly believe that this species out-thinks the hunter, showing real intellect. It expects an attacked baitfish to behave to a defined pattern. If that behaviour varies from the norm, *Ziphias gladius* leaves it well alone!

Algarve . . . and an extraordinary fish

Joined by Leslie Moncrieff and a party of London anglers, I moved on from Sesimbra, down to the southern coast, to what has now become the holiday Mecca for many Europeans. The Algarve had long been a noted sportfishing

An immature mako shark, lassoed in Leslie's trace while trying to swallow a bait that was almost as big as itself. Only nylon, used to tie the bait to the hook, held it against the hook.

area, so we headed for Cape St Vincent, the rocky headland that provides a sharp corner to Portugal. Here many tidal and ocean current influences cause quite a number of interesting species to gather. Thirty miles off the coast is a noted 'nursery' for mako shark. Les Moncrieff and I had ten or more small fish that weighed around 50–60 lb. They are ever present, feeding on pelagic baitfish.

The fishing that we really wanted to do, however, was over a reef, off Punta Pontal, that lay about 20 miles north of the Cape. Local commercial fishers told us that they were always losing long-lines set close to the reef. We had no common language but with a few words of French and much waving of hands the men of Sagres were able to indicate that enormous fish were robbing their lines. Now and then, they had felt them actually tethered on the line but had lost them, without getting a glimpse, as they began to haul.

I drew a number of fish outlines on the cafe's paper tablecloth, but to each drawing there was a quick shake of the head, indicating that my guess at the fish's identity was wrong. Finally, I drew a skate shape. Immediately the fishermen nodded but one chap, grabbing my pencil, made a few additions to the tail and mouth areas of the sketches, while muttering 'braai mante'. We reasoned that they thought the fish were manta rays. Now, books about big fish will tell you that manta rays are plankton feeders that do not feed on fish. It appeared that the books could be wrong. . . .

Our hosts insisted that the time to fish for the rays, and on this reef particularly, was at night. So, plans were made for such a venture.

We were a little unfortunate with our choice of skipper. He owned a huge ex-big-game boat that had come from the Bahamas. What he lacked in local knowledge about the coast, reefs and other dangers he made up for with speed. Nothing would deter the guy from going full chat up the coast in pitch darkness! To avoid trouble, Les took himself out on the forward decking to listen for the reef. We both thought that the skipper's reliance on his spotlights, to see the small amount of exposed rock, was a trifle misplaced.

Luckily, Les heard the crashing surf long before our skipper saw anything and made it quite clear that 20 knots was okay out at sea but not inshore where we were headed.

We had to anchor up to the leeward side of the reef. The bulk of our boat took too much wind on the drift, which meant that our first efforts to keep station were fruitless. The tackle had been organized back in the comfort of our hotel room: 50-lb class rods, multipliers with braided line and 250-lb wire traces to 10/0 hooks. We had an array of suitable fishbait, all fresh and filleted.

First drop down was a surprise. Although only about 40 yards from the reeftop, there was 20 fathoms of water beneath the keel. Down went everybody's bait to settle at the base of the undersea cliff. We had early bites, mostly nibbles from small fish, and then Les hooked a larger fish and brought it slowly up through the depths. It fought like a conger, but was actually a moray eel of about 20 lbs, with brown marbled flanks and a beaked head. That's when the fun started. Immediately we lost both the skipper and his local crewman, who took one look at the eel and scurried away below deck to the safety of the saloon. Obviously they considered morays to be too dangerous to handle. So we did the unhooking job ourselves.

We soon had moray, with a sprinkling of conger eels, coming aboard regularly. The wet fish well, intended for livebaits, became our enclosed fish box. The skipper paid one visit to see how things were going but the sight of so many eels proved too much for his delicate stomach! The first sign of anything out of the ordinary came as Bill Martin hauled yet another eel toward the boat. There was a terrific pull on the line and then nothing. . . .

Winding his gear in, he shouted that he had no weight at all. As the terminal trace came within the glare of our decklights, we could see the end of a frayed wire trace, which Les, who was about to rebait his rig, at once removed. He began fashioning a much heavier length of trace, and in due course a rig with 500-lb wire was quickly baited and lowered to the seabed.

It took only about ten minutes before he had an enormous take. The rod slammed over the gunwale and then straightened. Another trace came aboard bitten through, or to be more precise, severed.

These fishermen are cutting off the bill from a swordfish . . . for sale to a tourist! The fish itself is bound for the tables of hotels along the Algarve – a new holiday destination in those days.

The analysis started. What could the fish be? Sharks were discounted because there was no preliminary nodding of the rod tip or any attempt to run with the bait. The fish, whatever it was, had grabbed the bait in its mouth and that was enough to part cable-laid wire!

The truth is we never did succeed even in getting a sight of that fish, although we had another three or four instances of its tremendous strength.

We finished our night's fishing with almost 100 eels. The feat was duly recognized by both our skipper and his crewhand. The following morning, when we arrived for a new day's fishing, we learned that the 'priceless pair' had sold the eels, *having made certain they were dead*, to make themselves a handsome profit in the early morning fishmarket!

CHAPTER FOUR

A Baptism of Fire

WALES

When people ask me at angling talk shows to nominate my favourite fish, I often sense that what they really want to know is which species I regard as the acme of sportfishing and whether my choice agrees with their own.

Sea fishing is and, I suppose, always will be my first love. It isn't a matter of size, just the fact that saltwater has to enter the argument! Over the years my answer to any questioner has always been the same: pollack and porbeagle!

One other species must come into consideration when fishing into shallow

water from the beach is concerned, namely tope with their capacity to tear the last ounce of power from the tackle and test the angler's ability to use his gear. And if you say that there aren't many established shore angling marks for tope – you are quite right!

I didn't find the shore mark where I learned my shoreline toping trade. That was left to Clive Gammon, who telephoned me from Swansea, suggesting that if I got off my butt and took the train to Wales, I might just find the trip worthwhile. Apparently Clive and his pal Jim Griffiths, while bass fishing, had lost tackle and fish to something that hit them hard and successfully from the beach at Broughton. When told of the venue, I had no idea where it was. The name sounded Welsh, though Clive simply said that it was near 'Slash', later identified as Llanelli!

Regular shorefishing forays had apparently established both bass and mullet making a constant, upstream journey into the tidal estuary of the Loughor; and flounders, too, were plentiful. Yet while fishing the bottom with worms, Clive and Jim had lost fish to fearful tearing runs that could not have come from any of the three expected types of estuary fish. Eventually,

Two tope anglers, travelling light, strike out across the sands of Broughton Bay toward the channels that slice the flat sands at the low tidal phase.

one of the runs was held on a simple, nylon paternoster, and after a prolonged fight a small tope had been drawn into the shallow water of the channel. From that one fish came a new and hectic shore angling experience.

In those days not everybody possessed a car as fishing transport. Clive owned a rugged Landrover which trekked around South Wales beaches, climbing the dunes and making long forays across countless storm beaches in search of the elusive bass. The lads explained that the ebb tide took the water a very long way out, so I expected to be carried in Clive's wagon to the waterside, but I was wrong; here was one shore angling interlude that had to be undertaken on foot, and as I topped the dunes on this first day's toping I could understand why. Between us and the water there were areas of very soft, drifting sand and small channels.

The saltwater shone, beckoning in the distance, for the tide was right out and looked to be miles from where we had our first glimpse of the estuary and the layout of channels that cut the sands. Apart from my camera case, there was little to carry, just simple rod set-ups; multipliers and 18-lb line, a few 6-ounce leads and short wire traces to 6/0 hooks, across our shoulders. Clive had the bait, which he wouldn't show me. Obviously, I thought, it's fish but why the secrecy?

All was revealed when we finally reached the sea. Clive and Jim had put up with all manner of frustration over the provision of fresh hookbaits. The Swansea fishmongers had only stale mackerel or extremely soft herring when they called. Experiment proved neither to be reliable for the former had little run-producing power and the latter cast off the hook too easily, despite their efforts to tie it on. Then they hit on the answer – Tesco! The supermarket sold an extensive range of frozen food ready packed for convenient carriage to our shore mark!

Clive's choice for the perfect tope bait was frozen plaice fillets, all of uniform size and weight. Staying well frozen till we hit the beach, the fillets could be mounted on the hook and easily secured with elasticated thread. They would sail through the air, giving us distance. No mess, just super function!

Our arrival at the channel coincided with the young flood. Incoming water flow was fairly gentle, probably because the estuary is fairly wide. Nobody knew which channel might be the most productive for tope; we could only fish the nearest to the hard sand and take our chance. Clive projected an hour's wait before there would be any action. A few mullet passed us, finning their way upstream and the odd plopping sound suggested that there may have been feeding bass on the same journey.

The baiting and casting processes were new to me. We fashioned running leger rigs with fairly short wire traces. Mine was about 4 feet long, which is about all I can cope with when the weight has to be wound to the tip. Clive admitted that there were times, especially in the face of a powerful head wind, when he was forced to use a trace of only 2 feet, and he didn't lose fish. Of one thing he was certain; the trace should be new for each fishing outing. He hated nylon-covered wire because it so often rusted beneath the plastic covering, and this went undetected until a hard pull severed the trace. I believe that he even went to the trouble of having wire traces soldered up properly! We had 6/o Model Perfect hooks, in those days highly regarded for the larger sea fish, although today they would seem very thick in the wire. The size was sufficient, since a hookhold would rarely come adrift once the fish was truly on. Clive insisted on hooks being almost totally enclosed within the bait, with only a minimum of hookpoint allowed to protrude.

The most difficult thing to cope with was the need for a lot of line. My baby Penn Squidder 146 multiplier had a normal casting capacity of about 210 yards of 18-lb nylon, and I was told that every yard might be needed. I could have tackled up with a large fixed-spool reel but I have no love for them.

Thanks to a lot of Welsh sea anglers who had put in many hours of hard fishing, a pattern had emerged which involved wading into the shallow water, casting and then gradually walking back as the flood tide moved in. This often meant that one would have over 300 yards of line out. Needless to say, many of the lads used big centrepin reels, capable of holding 300–400 yards of line. I had crammed on as much nylon as my spool would carry. This made casting difficult, what with the free-wheeling of a heavy spool, yet it gave the recommended safety margin.

Tope are renowned for picking up a bait and running off before attempting to swallow it. In shallow water, such as we had before us, fish could swim at speed to the horizon. If one tope could come in to the channel, many more might follow, which meant competition for food, suggesting that the tope finding the bait must get away fast to protect its meal. Although I expected positive bites, both Clive and Jim had discovered that tope, in the shallow water of the estuary, were highly suspicious of their baits. Often the fish would mouth a bait, drop it for minutes, then come back to it again.

Our first fish did just that. After over an hour's wait, there came a few telltale clicks from Clive's ratchet, then silence for several minutes before the reel began to scream as the line was torn off at a great rate of knots. He picked the rod out of its rest, pointing the tip toward the direction of the flowing line. Nylon had literally disappeared from the spool: at least 50 yards was run off before any sign of slowing. The tope stopped momentarily, then began a second, sporadic flight.

As the run developed, Clive flipped the reel into gear, whipped the rod back in a hefty strike and brought the tip down to a fish-following angle. At the same time he knocked the ratchet off, as we had developed an aversion to the harsh noise seemingly welcomed by many anglers.

It is always hard to describe accurately just how far a fish runs, but I would suggest that the tope went for at least 100 yards before turning against the pressure of the drag, and this augmented by Clive's use of his thumbs. In fact, the applied pressure from the drag was slight compared to that which could be instantly added by the angler. Then it was a battle to recover line, while guarding against the shorter rushes made by the fish. Gradually, but very slowly, he regained some line on to the spool.

As the fight drew closer, the tope, to our surprise, came to the surface, something it rarely does when fighting in any sort of real depth. It began a kind of porpoising along the top of the water. Possibly it had been disorientated by the lack of depth and the power of the strong sunlight.

It took Clive about ten minutes in all to get his first tope to the sandy shallows. Jim thought about removing socks and boots if needed, ready to tail the fish on to the hard sand. A quick movement from behind, a confident grasp of the tail wrist, and the job was done. A tope of 30 lbs or so lay writhing before us. Despite a mass of sea lice on its upper caudal fin and behind the eyes, the fish was a thing of beauty.

Hook extraction was a doddle: lightly lip-hooked, it took only one twist of the pliers to remove the iron from the gristly jaw. Then, after a quick photograph, the first fish was slid back into the clouded waters of the channel.

We had to wait quite a while for any further action, and it came again to Gammon. This time, aware of my lack of experience in toping from the shore, he picked the rod up, knocked the ratchet off and thrust it into my hands, shouting, 'Do something about that, Prichard!'

Very gentlemanly of him, as I now realize, but slightly disconcerting at that moment! I had no time to think, although my immediate reaction was to slacken off the clutch a bit more, given the fact that the fish's strength of fight and speed through the water were going to be totally new to me. I enjoyed those initial minutes more for the novel experience than for the fight, which became one long, drawn out run. Finally, with a little help from both thumbs, I got the tope under some sort of control. It slowed, stopped and then slowly began to move again. 'Hit it!' roared Clive, and I did, holding the rod high in its curve to make certain that the line was tight to the fish.

I have had some fairly large fish from the beach, cod in heavy winter water and bass in tumbling surf, but that first tope was something else! It ran, came fast toward me and then slewed away to race downtide. One second I was retrieving line and the next moment nylon was peeling off the spool like there was no tomorrow. The rod didn't give me much help or control, as a modern one would have done. In the early 1960s we had little choice; apart from a glassfibre rod of about 11 feet, that cast leads of 4–5 oz, there was little else to be had. A bit floppy, though ideal for throwing a soft crab to bass, Clive's rod hadn't the steel to impose itself on tope, so the battle was protracted yet enjoyable. Every movement of the fish was telegraphed back down the line, most of its activities being relayed to me as a running commentary from my companions who were running up and down the channel-side, keeping pace with the fish as it sliced nylon through the surface.

Jim Griffiths grabs for the tail and a Welsh tope heads for the hard
sand. Even the strong fight offshore to shed the hook did not prevent
a battle in the last few inches of water!

I started to get a little line back after about ten minutes. Not much but
enough to indicate that I was winning. Soon it became apparent that the fish
was seesawing to and fro, in an arc. It ran about until it almost had its nose on
the beach, turned, and then swam round the arc of its tether to reach the sand
again. I put on a little more pressure but the nylon started singing. Clive
shouted gleefully it must be a sizable tope.

We saw it together. It came up and cruised the surface 30 yards out in the
stream. And it was big! What with trembling and not wanting to appear too

I felt quite pleased with myself . . . after all, the rod was Gammon's
and the fish was mine! Tope fishing from the shore was a new and
exhilarating experience.

much of a tyro, I took rather more time and care than was really necessary
over the last few minutes before the fish nosed into the shallows. Clive
grabbed it and I had a near 40 pounder, from the beach, to my credit. Despite
repeated attempts on shorelines said to be visited by massive fish, that was
the first and only time that such a tope has come to my bait, and I wouldn't
have missed it for anything!

CHAPTER FIVE

Whisky and Driva

SCANDINAVIA

My longing to visit Norway started in my school years with history lessons concerned with Vikings and the Norse Sagas. Later, when travelling around in northern Europe, these ancient people and their wanderings always seemed to crop up in conversation or provide the inspiration for a story.

The Orkneys, Shetlands, Hebrides, practically the whole of Ireland and many parts of England had been deeply affected by Norsemen. They had passed on their culture, named towns and villages and left stories, handed down over generations, of wild invaders who smashed their way across the northern world. Today, fishing in some of the more outlying places, you see local boats that show a sharp-prowed Nordic influence, and even the trinkets sold in tourists' craft shops still bear the stamp of these northern seafaring warriors.

Invited to go to the heart of Norway, I grabbed at the chance. There was a salmon fishing story to be had on the River Driva, said to be Norway's number two for catches. The journey itself was eventful: leaving London Airport, after the usual delay, Clive Gammon and I feared that we might miss the connecting flight. But a word to the cabin staff resulted in the pilot passing our problem, by radio, to the airport at Bergen. They promised to hold the ongoing flight till our arrival. Sure enough, when we finally landed in Norway, there was the up-country aircraft sitting on the tarmac, with its smiling passengers patiently waiting to greet two intrepid British anglers, three-quarters of an hour late! Obliged to transfer all the gear from one aircraft to the other, we never did see the inside of the immigration or customs halls.

We flew on from Bergen to Vigra, then transferred to a small slipway on the coast. Soon we were off by hovercraft in a flurry of spray, racing up a long fjord from the airfield which lay on an offshore island, to Molde. Kristian Fahlstrom, our Norwegian host who had spent many months organizing the trip, met us and brought us by car to Sunndalsora, a small modern town lying below the Littledal range of towering mountain peaks.

Seeking information about the fishing, in our initial conversation with the local experts, brought a disappointment. Weather conditions weren't right for salmon fishing but our hosts wondered if we could possibly make do with seatrout! Not a bad alternative, Clive being a Welshman brought up on fishing

The River Driva at
Sunndalsora. The
mountains, surging water
and open sky provided a
tremendous backcloth to our
first experience of Norway
and its fishing.

his native rivers for the species. We both considered that seatrout were a far better angling proposition, we could hardly wait.

The Norwegians got us out to the river in the late evening. Apparently there was a daily rise and fall in the Driva's water level. Daytime temperatures, of around the high 8os F., produced snowmelt in the mountains which brought higher water in the hours of true daylight. By evening the flow of water slackened away and trout began to run the river. From then until the sun rose again over the mountains, local fishers came to the river.

Slightly journey-fatigued, we stumbled across the pebbles to wade into the shallow but wide pool. All traces of tiredness soon disappeared as the icy water covered our feet. The Driva is a huge river and there was no way in which it could be covered, across the mainstream, with a fly. Enquiries had established that fish ran the broad water along several paths. Luckily, one of the favourite routes was on our side of the river. Signs of travelling fish were evident, with mighty splashes within a few yards of the pebbly shore telling us that the run was on! Both Gammon and I had our rods equipped with floating lines, Clive using a 10-foot cane rod while I wanted the ease of casting with my 11-foot double-hander. He tied on a smallish, salmon fly, a Silver Doctor as I remember, and I chose a minnow fly, lightly leaded at the head, which had been tied back in London by Geoffrey Bucknall specially for the trip. We'd been told, quite forcibly, that your flies had to scrape the pebbles. Apparently the running trout rarely rose in the shallow water, only about 18 inches deep, to a surface-swimming lure.

Concentration was broken by the appearance of a satellite glowing, comet-like, as it skimmed across the heavens. Back in Britain we would always choose to fish well after dark, sometimes in pitch blackness. In the Sunndal valley we could see all about us, and long after the sun had gone I could easily

Leaded minnows, tied by Geoffrey Bucknall back in London specially for my trip to Norway, proved ideal to fish an inch or so above the riverbed in powerful water.

read the engraved figures on my lenses or pick out figures moving at the chalet farmhouses, high up on the mountainsides. It is extremely difficult to describe fishing under the midnight sun – it has to be experienced.

Starting to cast at the head of a massive pool, I watched countless fish leaping clear of the water as they came upriver. I made repeated casts with my double-handed rod, bringing the fly around in a wide sweep that covered the area of fish activity. Getting the smallest of pulls, I threw the rod back to feel nothing, although it may have been a momentary snatch as the fly hit a stone on the riverbed. At least, I thought, the lure is in the right spot.

A shout from Clive told me that he had positive contact with his first Driva seatrout. Anxious to get pictures, I waded out and hurried along the pebbly shore to where he had retreated out from the river. I made a mistake by badly misjudging the available amount of light. Although I could see Clive clearly, the needle of my exposure meter refused to budge from zero, so back to my rod I went.

Another cast to the fast water that marked my target area produced yet another slight snatch on the line. This can't be right, I thought, and ran through advice Herbert Normington had given me when fishing seatrout on a water far away in Cumberland. 'Strike quickly at anything,' was his maxim. After a few more fruitless casts I did get the tiniest of trembles back through the line. Lifting hard on the rod, I knew that I had him.

The fish came out of the water in a jerking, head-shaking jump. Droplets of water spun around as the trout performed a wriggling climb, before walloping back into the river. For five minutes I enjoyed a series of runs and leaps across the river and upstream of where I stood trembling. Making for the stony shore, carefully feeling for sound footholds, I stumbled around, finding it difficult to keep my feet where there was any sort of current flow over smooth, round pebbles. My fish was quietening and I managed to recover some line to the reel. By now all jumping activity had ceased; in fact, the fish drifted below me to lie dormant in the flow. So I walked it out on to the shingle.

I can't claim that the trout was massive . . . but it was the largest I'd ever had! Four pounds of muscle, silver-scaled and thick-bodied. Feeling more than pleased with myself, I tottered through the half-light to exchange experiences with Clive and Kristian. Arriving downstream, I was surprised to find three or four hazy figures gathered on the shore, in the shadow of the low trees. Apparently word had got round that Gammon had a bottle of whisky with him, a pretty rare sight in Norway! This, supplemented by the glass jammed into the top of his waders, brought a new drink into being: a scoop of ice-cold river water, with a splash of Scottish spirit, became a 'Whisky and Driva'!

It was the habit of the local farmers to drift down to the river most nights. Equipped with bamboo rods, at least 20 feet long, they would cast for a fish

Clive's fish from the Driva proved to be all that we had been promised!
And this one came in the glare of noonday sunlight, though most
seatrout are taken in the dark hours.

under the brightly lit sky, often taking a salmon as well as the freshly run trout. Sleeping hours were dictated by the run of fish in the river. We found ourselves adopting a similar regime. Back to bed at five or six in the morning, sleep till after midday, then up to play tourist, driving high in the mountains, to the flat tundra where reindeer graze the mosses and enormous mosquitoes dive in disciplined squadrons to plague both man and beast.

In the early evening we made courtesy calls on farmers, our fishing companions of the night, to enjoy huge bowls of fresh strawberries covered with cream. We learned that one could fish during the day but the hours after midnight were best. Only the serious salmon angler would ply his trade in the heat of the day. I found myself having to plead with my two friends to help me out, by fishing during the day when I had enough light to produce photographs. They willingly complied, and were astonished to find that the seatrout were still running and prepared to take their flies. So we caught fish in tremendous heat and under extremely bright light, where only a foot or so of water covered the riverbed.

Later in the week's fishing we went on to catch small, wild brown trout in the tiny mountain streams. Inevitably Clive and I had to taste the saltwater angling. Kristian Fahlstrom's home town was at Kristiansund Nord. There in deepwater, among rocky offshore islands we treated ourselves to some cod bashing. The area was associated with commercial halibut fishing, done on longlines, although these fish eluded us. I have since wondered whether Norway's fishing remains as I remember it, or if they are experiencing similar pressures to our own. Perhaps I'll find the cash to make a return journey to the Northland before too long – and next time they may find a moment to stamp my passport!

Ansager interlude

There was a time when fishermen could be forgiven for thinking that Denmark had only one river! The Guden was held to be supreme for its fish numbers and had gained notoriety when several UK match sponsors chose the river to fish their respective championships. I think it was toward the end of the 1960s that I first went across the North Sea to Jutland to try the Guden for myself. It was big, something like the Trent where it flows through the countryside downstream of Nottingham. The Guden appeared to have the same sort of surface speed, the depth, in many places, was similar, yet it was certainly different. The water was clean, with none of the telltale signs of pollution which were beginning to show on rivers that flowed through Britain's industrial heartland.

Denmark seemed to have all the ingredients for perfect coarse fishing and, after a few days on the Guden, I went off to the centre of Jutland to find other waters. Allen Edwards and Dennis Burgess made up the party on this exploratory trip. Ken Sutton, a former secretary of the ACA, was to introduce us to two lesser streams, the Ansager and Grindsted, both lush waterways that joined a few miles below the town of Grindsted. While crossing the North Sea, on a huge DFDS ferry, Ken had described the quality of roach to be caught. He hinted, too, that the size of resident dace might also surprise us.

This was to be Allen's trip; coming from Nottingham, he was the expert on flowing streams. Taking only one look at the Ansager, he told us that this was long-trotting country. That put me 'out of the park' straight away. My experience, limited as it was then to stillwaters and an occasional visit to slow-running East Anglian rivers, wouldn't give me much of a chance to get the best of our promised roach. I had visions of centrepin reels, but I needn't have worried. Edwards is the sort of bloke who provides you with all that is necessary, plus enough advice to get you fish, before setting off alone to his own preselected hotspot!

I fished for a few hours, caught some roach with difficulty yet couldn't get too interested. I wanted to know what was happening upstream, so I took a stroll along the waterside, through soft meadows to where he sat half-hidden behind a stand of reed. I stood behind Allen for a long time during his day on the Ansager, and though it was easy to see why he had elected to fish that particular swim (it reeked of fish), I was mainly interested in the way he went about it. The river came from his right, swung into a large bay to his left and then continued flowing downstream, taking a slight bend to the right.

He couldn't trot down along a straight line because of the influence of the large eddy that formed within the bay. The roach proved not to be lying at the side of the eddy, but rather further downstream where the bulk of the flow left the bay to squeeze through a narrow entrance to the next stretch of river. I would have cast float tackle to a point alongside the eddy, beginning a trot where the flow was starting to straighten. Allen didn't do that at all. . . .

He began his trot within a few yards of where he sat, about a couple of rod lengths beyond the fringe of reed that gave him superb cover. His float tackle would hit the water, the float cocked and the tackle had time to settle before arriving anywhere near the waiting fish. I believe that Allen's success on that day was that his bait swung out from the eddy in a perfectly natural way – just as food drifting within the current would behave – and precisely as waiting fish expected.

It was quite a long trot to the roach, at least 30 yards, maybe longer. Throughout the session I saw very few strikes fail to connect. Each fish came back through the current fairly steadily for the first few yards, only appearing to fight the power of the rod when it drew alongside the eddy in the stream. That was another of Allen's successes; at no time were hooked fish upsetting the shoal from which they were drawn!

The catch was close to 100 lbs and Allen, in his quiet way, told me that he thought there were at least twelve fish that would weigh over two pounds

My first ever two-pound roach! A fish from the junction of the Rivers
Ansager and Grindsted where a quiet backwater lay out of the full
pressure of the current.

among the catch. Typically, he was under-estimating the quality of the bag,
for I believe that there were far more two pounders in the net.

I am proud to say that I have a plaque on which are mounted a matched pair
of Ansager roach. Allen took just two fish back to the university in Nottingham. Before technicians set up the fish there, they made plaster casts of the
perfectly scaled roach so that each of us could have a memento enabling us to
share in his angling interlude on the Ansager River, my choice as Denmark's
finest coarse fishery.

CHAPTER SIX

Where The Ocean meets The Sky

IRELAND

For years shore anglers have chosen the long yellow strands of the Dingle Peninsula as their favourite fishing spot. High among the many reasons must be the sheer exhilaration of being pounded by the streaming Atlantic surf of these storm beaches. Built up by mid-ocean storms, the creaming breakers roll steadily in to the smooth sands, subsiding into flat tables of water that glide up on to the strand. In the breakers, within sight of an angler, the scaly bass flashes to and fro in the glistening water, constantly searching for worms and sandeels forced out from the sand as each curling wave spends its energy on the beach.

Surf fishing has an added ingredient for the men who fish the littoral waters of Ireland's west coast. Standing in the moving water, watching and feeling the line as each rolling line of surf breaks around protective waders, the angler is keenly aware that he is only a small part of the ecosystem, surrounded by other life forms. Power is the key to the marine world – the power of the ocean and the wild winds that drive the huge surface swells in to pound the shoreline. Tide streams and currents are mere children of that awesome force formed so far off in tropical and arctic waters. Wading into the rushing water to let loose a baited rig, one feels so tiny and alone in a world dominated by the sea and the endless sky.

Many years ago, driving out from Tralee, I had my first glimpse of the golden sands that ring Brandon Bay. There on the north side of the peninsula, beyond the tiny hamlet of Castlegregory, where a finger of sand dunes juts out to a mass of tiny, rocky islands, the strands lie open to the sea. At the western end of miles of beach, the mighty hump of St Brendan's mountain marks the beginning of a series of indented bays that shelter small, solitary whitewashed houses and stone jetties, from which the people of the peninsula set out to fish.

Dingle spells bass, which have a natural liking for clean, clear water that has been warmed by currents spilling off from the North Atlantic Drift. It is one of those rare shorefishing locations where bass can be found in any month of the

year, although their average size has never been very high. My largest
weighed 8½ lbs and I haven't often seen bigger fish from that part of the
south-west. This may be because bass, in western areas, feed on the open
grounds in fairly wild water; perhaps their life is one of constant swimming
activity and battle against the elements. Bass found in harbours and stillwater
lagoons seem to attain larger body weight, suggesting that the life of a
scavenger, feeding on shore crabs, sandeels and detritus, provides more
nutrition with less energy expended.

There is one particular day that I shall long remember. It started with a
protracted bait-digging session at Clogharne, made difficult by an incoming
tide that continuously forced us to retreat from the sand–mud mixture that
held the larger lugworm to weeded, shallow areas which produced only
stringy worms, though we added a few useful clams to the bait bucket. We
washed our worms, cleaning them in the rush of fresh, tidal water, then
covered the wriggling mass with bladderwrack, as a necessary precaution
against the drying heat of a sun that promised a perfect Dingle day.

We had decided to fish the open strand at Kilcummin, reached by driving
back toward Castlegregory to where a stony boreen inclines seaward. This
shore mark is identified by a solitary wooden post, jutting out from the sand at

Digging on the Clogharne lugworm beds – a two-man job. Gammon
handled the fork, while Ian Gillespie did the picking. He rarely
missed a rapidly burrowing worm!

low tide, said to mark the remains of an early wreck. A shallow stream follows the lane down to the shore and there it spills on to the gently sloping sand.

We spread ourselves out at either side of the post. Clive Gammon, an extremely knowledgeable bass angler who now lives and works in America, chose his hotspot next to the freshwater flowing over the beach, muttering that 'bass are always to be found around freshwater running off the land'. Kevin Linnane was first out into the surf, making purposeful strides against the pressure of the breakers. He always liked to be in thigh-deep surf, where he could gain the extra few yards to his casting – at the risk of a wet backside. I must confess that I have a natural aversion to being soaked, especially at the junction of my legs, so I try to find a fishing position where current pulls the bait round with strength. I know that it can be hard to hold the ground, even when using a griplead, but bass seem to search for food where the water is wildest.

Our arrival coincided with the last hour or so of the flood, perhaps not the best time to begin a bassing session, yet bites came almost immediately. Kevin, who was probably fishing farthest out from the sand, struck hard. Moving back quickly, with a faint shout on the breeze to tell us that he was 'in', Kev picked up the slackish line that bellied between him and the fish. His rod arched over, then straightened, as each rolling breaker put its pressure against the moving bass. I have always found it difficult to maintain that 'tight line contact' that is vital in keeping a strong fish headed my way in tumbling water. Kevin's fish seemed a good one, so we all put our rods into rests and ran along the shallows to get a sight of the first of the season's Dingle bass. It played hard in the last 20 yards of flat water, careering sideways along the water table with vigorous head-shaking, intended to dislodge the hook.

With a practised hand, born of catching hundreds of bass in his time, Kevin played the fish on the rod. Then it lay, floundering, in a few inches of water ahead of his boots. A couple of strides and Kev put himself between the bass and the incoming line of surf – always a bright thing to do with a fish that, in its last desperate lunge, can shake off from the hook. The usual congratulations were proffered and a few hands stretched out to give the hard-scaled body a purposeful rub – establishing a kind of affinity between man and the highly prized quarry!

Back we all trooped to our respective rods, which stood like sentries in their rests. Some of us immediately took the rods down to hold them tightly across our chests. I admit to enjoying holding my bassrod throughout a tide of fishing. Clive Gammon, during my nursery days when I fished alongside him in West Wales, convinced me of the value of always holding the rod with the nylon crooked over my little finger. He believed in an intimate contact with the slightest vibration that might be transmitted back along the reel line – almost willing fish on to his bait!

Bass fishing can certainly be tiring, what with the constant to and fro of the

Ian Gillespie, fingers ever ready for a bite, and Kevin Linnane (right)
check the number on a tagged bass, before returning it to the gentle,
rolling breakers of Brandon Bay.

water that shifts fine sand, undermining one's waders and enforcing a change
of stance after each table of water weakens and begins to run back to join the
surf. Most times I prefer to stand facing the breakers, hoping to see birds
working the surf or, more rarely, actually to catch a glimpse of bass swimming
along inside the turning wave. As this stance becomes tiring, I turn my back
on the sea, still holding the rod across my chest. From this position it is much
easier to react to a solid bite. One can strike by punching the rod away and at
the same time take up slack line with a couple of hasty strides, up the strand,
toward dry sand.

Within the hour the tide started to ebb, with a noticeable slackening of
power. The turning breakers eased, although a slight off-the-water breeze
kept a ready curl to the rolling surflines. I do not much enjoy fishing on an ebb
tide. On surf beaches, it never seems to yield more than a few schoolies and
flounders – yet, the ebb is still far better than a surfless day!

We fished for another hour or so before Dennis Burgess, a newcomer to the
Kerry sands, gave a shout and turned to display a quizzical grin, as if seeking
confirmation that his detected bite was from a bass. It was his first time in
Dingle and his first bass fishing session. We had all lectured him on the wide

Dennis Burgess with his first bass, a fish from Stradbally that weighed
a little over 8 lbs. This was above average size for bass of the Dingle
Peninsula.

variety of bites that he could expect, and the trembling tweak he'd experienced was hardly the promised lusty wallop that we had all assured him
spelled bass. As soon as his line tightened, however, Dennis himself realized
that this was no flounder, or even a school bass. Once again an audience grew
behind the angler as the fight progressed. Inundated with ribaldry, and an
element of advice, most of it useless to a tyro bass angler, he did the right
thing by keeping a tight line to the fish that swam 60 yards out in the rough
water.

It is always a pleasure to watch a fisherman handle a fish well. This battle
was no exception. Dennis may not have caught a bass before but he had
mastered many good winter cod and difficult freshwater species. Another
and possibly more crucial thrill in bassfishing is getting the first glimpse of the
fish, watching it respond both to the pressure on its head and the surge of
water rolling landwards. Dennis's fish surfaced and ran along the edge of a
turning breaker as though it was surfing, speeding from one breaker to the
next, disappearing momentarily into the troughs.

Roars of 'tight line' issued from the gallery, while I was busy with my
camera, trying for the opportunity of a picture of the fish cutting through the
water tables. Like seconds in a boxer's corner, the lads kept up their chatter
until, in a few inches of creaming water, Dennis was able to reach down and
lift his first bass by the gillcase. Amid the excitement he did not notice that he
had cut himself badly on the sharp spine on the fish's gillcase. The fish
weighed 8 lbs 4 oz – a creditable performance and a splendid beginning to
Den's bassfishing career.

A few smaller bass came our way on the weakening ebb tide, but we soon
agreed to leave the strand until the beginning of the evening flood. Les
Moncrieff, Dennis and I decided to fish later in the day somewhere in the area
beneath the sand dunes at Stradbally. Clive Gammon, with Kevin Linnane
and Ian Gillespie, were making their plans to fish at Inch, a west-facing storm
beach that juts out at right angles into Dingle Bay. This strand had always
proved reliable for a catch of bass when there was anything like a tickle of surf
running. After a leisurely meal in the village, we divided into two parties and
left for our respective fishings.

Les had chosen our fishing spot on the basis that Stradbally was a 'sharp
corner' of Brandon Bay. Evidence of the sweeping, tidal action was indicated
by the rounded pebbles that are only found on this part of the 14-mile-long
strand. As Clive remarked: 'There is only one beach in Kerry that looks like
Dungeness – and Moncrieff has found it!'

We expected fish fry and other littoral-water food to be driven into
Stradbally. Feeding bass should have been grouped up as the evening light
dwindled and the flood got under way. As it turned out, I waited for a hour
before the first distinct knock came, from a smallish bass, a schoolie that
weighed a couple of pounds. In the next hour, before true darkness, each of

Three satisfied shore anglers with the fruits of their labours. As the light went, so the surf faded to a gentle turning wave pattern that suggested better fishing during the night.

us took many similar sized fish. Our flood tide, on the northern side of the peninsula, lacked the benefit of a wind behind it, so the offshore swell was gentle and only a soft tickle of surf ran on to the strand. In conditions like that I prefer to fish in the darkest hours, as I cannot ever remember having a good catch when there was practically no water movement. In daylight, with the added ingredient of bright sunshine, absence of breakers gives the angler no chance. In such circumstances bass stay out in deepwater that offers a darker environment, with increased security from predators. Only at night will these fish venture right up to the tidemark when there is only a slack surf.

In those days Leslie was unrivalled as a long-distance shorecaster. When he bent into a rod, he could outcast both Dennis and me by at least 40 yards – with bait on! Proof of his ability and his control of a multiplying reel, that lacked any of the modern breaking devices, came after dark. Even though we couldn't see the flight of his lead, we judged the trajectory by the sound made as the spindle rotated in its bearings. Suddenly he shouted that he had hooked a bass that wasn't behaving at all like the book said. In a couple of minutes he had the first of a dozen or so spurdogs lying on the sand. Since Dennis and I continued to catch bass for an hour or more without a sign of a spurdog ravaging our hookbaits, we concluded that Leslie's baits were fishing many yards beyond ours. I think that the crafty spurdogs were farther out than the bass, making sneaking runs into the shallow water to pick up the unwary fish that were too preoccupied with their own feeding in the shallows. When we opened our bass, they were filled with small sandeels and minute, partly digested creatures that felt like gritty sandhoppers.

By one o'clock in the morning we were just about ready to pack up the gear when a shout, from atop the dunes, heralded the arrival of the Inch fishers. They hadn't done so well; in fact, Clive admitted that they had ceased fishing early in favour of some convivial drinking 'behind the onion factory'. So, accompanied by our giggling companions, we left Stradbally for the warmth of our Castlegregory guesthouse.

*   *   *   *   *

As a postscript to this expedition, it is worth mentioning the research work done by Kevin Linnane in the course of his earlier professional life as a field officer with the Inland Fisheries Trust. That organization, now absorbed into the Central Fisheries Board, did much to control the sport, improve the freshwater fishing and provide anglers with vital information on fresh and saltwater fishing in Ireland. In the late 1960s Kevin was engaged in establishing the areas of bass populations and seasonal migratory habits. As part of that research he needed to catch a lot of bass on rod and line. Scales were required to indicate the fish's age group, and also reproductive organs to establish fecundity and spawning periods.

A tagged bass swims away through a table of shallow water. Who
knows where or when the fish might have been caught again. If it was
caught and the tag returned, the Inland Fisheries Trust would have
learned a great deal regarding its migratory behaviour and such growth
as the fish had made during its period of liberty.

Many of us were pressed into willing service as catchers for the Trust. We
took a lot of fish which were, quite rightly, sent to the scientists so that they
could learn more about the species. We hoped that the resultant scientific
papers would help to control commercial over-fishing and that anglers could
also share in the spread of definitive information to improve the lot of this
species. Alas, by the time the gathered information was available, bass
holding-grounds had been all but wiped clean by the trawlers. There are still
bass to catch, on the west coast of Ireland, but not in the numbers that were
previously caught nor in the places that were historically associated with this
splendid, fighting fish.

CHAPTER SEVEN

The Day of the Birds

IRELAND

Way off the tip of the Dingle Peninsula, where rugged cliffs jut arrogantly into the rolling Atlantic swell, lie the Blasket Islands. Windswept and treeless, the seven major islands are host to countless seabirds and the sheep of former human inhabitants who are now settled on the mainland of Kerry.

The Blaskets are separated from the bulk of Ireland by The Sound, a roiling, tempestuous mass of jumbled water that surges over reef and skerry. Beneath the heaving tide rip lies some of the foulest ground that I have ever fished over, a broken seabed that tore the belly from many a ship. I am told that at least two of King Philip's majestic Spanish galleons rent their oak planks there in Armada times, leaving a legacy of sunken treasure and, from the surviving sailors, a dark skin to many of the western population.

Sunset across Inishtooskert, the most northerly of the Blasket Islands. Though uninhabited throughout most of the year, a group of hardy folk are re-establishing a summertime community on Great Blasket.

To fish in such a place demands a lifetime of intimate knowledge of the wind and the ocean currents. Superficial expertise is of little use in combating the natural vagaries of this sea or in keeping yourself alive when the weather chooses to turn.

I once helped to plan a fishing holiday for the winners of the Guinness sea-angling competition. We needed to put twenty English sea fishers among the finest sport we could find. The party had to be divided between fishing from a boat and standing, thigh-deep, in the thrusting surf of the storm beaches. Dingle is one of the few venues that can provide both forms of sea angling, and which also offers something special when casting into deep-water from the rocky, Atlantic shore. So I made for Dingle without delay.

A traditional side-trawler lay chafing her ropes against the steep wall of the harbour. Her name was *Ard Ide* and Sean Brosnan was her skipper. Sean, a quietly spoken Kerryman, had a reputation for finding fish. His crewman, Paddy 'Bawn' Brosnan, had, in earlier years made an international reputation on the football field. With some trepidation I listed the species that the lads would like to catch, explaining to Sean that the winners of the competition were drawn from all parts of Britain with little common ground, as far as their home fishing was concerned. Brosnan smiled, gave a gentle nod of the head and promised not to disappoint them.

Sea fishing to a defined plan is a pretty tall order at any time but I was quietly confident that this man Brosnan knew exactly where and how to whet the appetites of the 'Guinness Brigade'! Before meeting the plane bringing the lads to Shannon, I spent my time searching out the nearest bait beds and in

Another of the shore fisher's change baits, a common otter shell *Lutraria lutraria* found washed out from the sand after a strong flood tide pounded the strand.

making a trip to view the Blasket Islands from the mountainous road that winds its precarious way around Slea Head.

Cloghane estuary proved to offer the best lugworm ground that I could possibly wish for. Vast acres of worm casts littered the drying flats and there was considerable evidence of the presence of clams (the sandgaper *Mya arenia*) – important change bait for the surfcaster. On this occasion the Guinness winners were not being asked to dig their own bait, for getting everybody started in the morning is always a problem with an 'organized' party of fishermen, so we had arranged for Pat Walsh, a Cloghane man, to dig for the party. Pat lives with his mother in a tiny cottage on the side of the road that sweeps around the muddy estuary. From his bedroom window he has a view of seascape and clouds that defies description – something that few cameras or artists can adequately capture!

My slow drive around the peninsula was fascinating. Every bend in the road demanded that I stop and take yet another photograph as the ever-changing vista of islands and sky unfolded. The height of the road above the sea gave that aerial view that is so necessary when defining the position of reefs and channels. Across the Sound I could see, shining in the early sunlight, the roofs of the tiny houses nestling among the ruins of earlier humble dwellings that dot the eastern slope of Great Blasket. Nobody lives permanently on the island these days but a wisp of smoke told of the summer residents who are endeavouring to lure overseas visitors, for just a few short weeks, to the peace and isolation of island life.

Planning done, the time came to meet with the winners as they poured from the Boeing 707 on to Shannon's tarmac. Although only a hundred miles or so, the journey westward to Dingle took ages – punctuated as it was by frequent stops at the quaint hostelries that line the road! Five hours saw us in Benners Hotel, excitedly talking of the morrow.

Morning was a difficult time, to say the least, as mountains of gear were sorted out. Tackle that should have been to hand was frantically sought among suitcases, pockets and anywhere else that a 1-lb weight could be hidden to avoid the surcharges that the airlines, in those days, were so fond of imposing. Finally, the boat party hit the quayside – only to find that *Ard Ide* was firmly glued to the harbour mud that an earlier start would have avoided. There on the harbour wall came the first lesson in 'Irish Time'. Sean, leaning from the wheelhouse window, suggested that the lads take their ease, look at the day and be prepared to leave in one hour, when the returning tide would give enough water to float us off and out through the marked channel to Dingle Bay. Conditioned to the trade union hours kept by some of the charter boats back home, the lads looked glum. They need not have worried because Dingle men will stay fishing until everybody cries enough!

Our first day's boat fishing was to be around the Blaskets, staying fairly close to the Sound where Sean had seen a massive shoal of mackerel on his

The seabirds, gannets, kittiwakes and fulmars, all around were telling us that we had fish beneath the boat, though only the gannets could see them below in the depths.

A gleaming dark-olive pollack . . . the supreme predator over the
pinnacles. It is my favourite fish from the cod family – possessing
incredible power and speed.

previous day's trawling. When only just past Ventry Harbour, we could see
clouds of birds working. Thousands of gannets, fulmars and kittiwakes flew
in tight circles as they scanned the sea below for the fish that would offer them
an hour's gorging. We passed in under Slea Head, keeping to the seaward
side of that fearsome chunk of jutting rock that pierces the water off Dunmore
Head. As though following the boat, the gannets and other oceanic birds
moved into the same troubled waters. Sean slowed the boat, indicating that
we all ought to have five minutes with the feathers to gather sufficient bait for
the day.

Mackerel were all around us. In fact, it was incredibly difficult to get the
sinkers much below a couple of fathoms as the weights could be felt bouncing
on the backs of fish that swarmed under *Ard Ide*'s keel. Everywhere there were
birds diving and skimming the waves while keeping up their incessant cries,
and within minutes there was enough mackerel to keep us all in fresh bait
forever!

Someone, forward on the bow of the boat, shouted that he was into a much
larger fish – something that moved fast and kept diving strongly. There was
the usual rush to witness the surfacing of what turned out to be a specimen
pollack. Obviously the arrival of the mackerel had brought the pollack up
from the reefs below. Feathered traces were hurriedly removed in favour of

single-hook flowing traces. With Paddy Bawn cutting mackerel lashes as fast as he could, we all dropped baits down to where the fish had been. For a few minutes nothing happened. The mackerel shoal had, in their frenzied rushing, passed from under the boat; but in they came again and the pollack were with them.

As *Ard Ide* drifted on the oily swell, pollack after pollack was hooked and made lunging rushes down to the seabed. We roared with laughter as some of the lads ran to and fro, along the side decks, desperate to stay in contact with fish that moved with fantastic speed. Rods were passed over and under each other in an effort to avoid tangles and losing the chance of a specimen fish. A

thin lash of bait I had dropped on the uptide side of the boat fell through the water unheeded by either species until it hit the rocky bottom. Mindful of the rough ground thereabouts, I took the precaution of winding in a couple of turns on the reel. Seconds later I had a savage pull to the lash of mackerel. Assuming it was another huge pollack, I struck hard to set the hook and lift the fish's head away from the foul ground. My fish, however, did not respond in quite the way that I had expected. It retaliated to the strike by yanking the rod over, tugging yards of line from the reel, and pulling the rod down to the gunwale. At first I thought the bite was in my imagination and that the lead had caught fast in the rocks below, with the pull coming as the boat drifted

Over went my rod and stayed in a compression curve far beyond that intended for the light-tackle blank! This tope took the bait among the rocks that litter the seabed in The Sound.

It is inevitable, at the seaward end of Dingle Bay, that vast shoals of spurdog move inshore to feed on the mackerel and, when boated, expect the sea angler to play midwife! (Top right) A spurdog pup emerging into the world. (Centre right) The fully-formed fish has absorbed its yolk sac. (Bottom right) Perfect in every way – and free to swim the Atlantic.

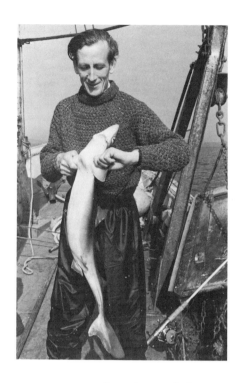

and lifted on the gentle swell, yet the movement seemed too fast and sharp to be caused by the boat's drift. The moving pressure stopped and then started again, this time with purpose, for the fish had altered its flight direction.

I put ten minutes hard work into that fight and, eventually, a tope broke the surface. Meanwhile, others were having a similar battle. It turned out that we had at least three tope on at the same time! Obviously the mackerel shoal had brought the pollack up from their usual haunts among the rock-strewn seabed and the tope, which would normally have been found out on the open sand bottom of Dingle Bay, had moved in to attack both mackerel and pollack alike. There we were with the richest angling opportunity that many of us had ever experienced in our fishing lives. Although Sean, our skipper, had led us to this fantastic mark, we owed our thanks to the birds whose keen vision had found the fish for us.

I have never seen such avian activity before or since. There were gannets diving within inches of the hull, oblivious of our presence as they sought to bring a fish up on each dive from 100 feet or more. Often the bird would grip the fish across its bill and only swallow it on regaining the surface. Swarms of lesser seafowl scurried around on the water's surface, fighting for oily scraps and becoming entangled in the nylon lines. It was one of nature's feeding frenzies!

Our angling activity proceeded in fits and starts, with everybody getting into good fish – tope and pollack – then losing contact as these predators followed hard on the trail of the vast shoal of mackerel. Either the Sound was being scoured by the mackerel for planktonic feed or the fish were circling around desperately trying to escape the attentions of the larger species. Once

before I had seen something similar, farther east, near Kinsale Old Head, when two killer whales sought to prevent the escape of a herd of porpoises that they had trapped in a rocky bay. Then, too, the birds had given the first clue to what was happening below the waves, as they circled the slaughter that they could see, and we could only imagine!

*   *   *   *   *

I remember another dramatic example of feeding frenzy which involved both birds and fish. One day in late spring I was tramping across the last of the boggy patches between the coast road and Doolin Strand in County Clare. Long before I reached the waterside my attention was drawn to the birds. Hundreds of gannets, accompanied by terns, kittiwakes and gulls were wheeling and diving down to strike into the shallow water only a few yards from the beach.

With brisk wind, the sea was boisterous. The splashing of birds and the thrusting bow-waves that sliced across the face of turning breakers indicated the presence of fish. At first I thought they were mackerel, feeding inshore. But then I saw larger, silver-scaled bodies that shouted bass! They seemed to be chasing a huge shoal of smaller fish that darted to and fro in their efforts to escape. The small fry, panicked either by the feeding bass or by the birds hitting the surface beyond the zone of predatory fish, had been forced tight up to the sand, hard into the roily water, from where there was no escape.

Bass were leaving the water in their frenzy to get at the whitebait. They actually leapt clear over the top of a creaming surf line to hit the water behind the white froth, which must surely have obscured vision of their intended meal. A heaven-sent fishing opportunity, you might think; but it didn't turn out like that.

Beach fishermen are conditioned to hurling wormbaits out into surf for bass. Rarely will you find spinning gear in their cars – and that was what I needed to get a bass to pause in its chase. All I had were worms and a few clams. I could easily reach the fish, in fact I could almost touch bass as they ripped into the fry in the last table of water thrown on to the strand. I tried, repeatedly, putting a legered bait into the feeding area, but it remained untouched, even when I was eventually reduced to casting and retrieving the worms in a fast, spinning-like fashion. Frustration wasn't the word for it – I could have cried!

CHAPTER EIGHT

Pike among the Chimney Tops

ENGLAND

Abberton reservoir lies in the north-east corner of Essex, a few miles from Colchester. The water rests in gentle folds in the soft, rolling landscape and, apart from supplying the vital needs of the county's population and industry, it contains a marvellous head of shoal fish and pike.

Not all of the water is available to anglers as a large area comprises a nature reserve for birds, both migratory and resident, demarcated by the road that runs along the top of the dam wall. The anglers of Abberton are lucky in that the reservoir contains coarse fish in abundance, with no trout to confuse the rules of specimen hunting!

I first went to Abberton in the early 1960s, invited by the late Ian Gillespie, who had unique permission to fish from the valve tower – unique in that there was no room for other people, and that we were fishing over 90 feet of water! Below, in the depths, was a 'drowned village', and often you could feel a spinning lure dragging across the top of an invisible cottage roof.

Special lures were necessary for spinning this situation. The spinner had to be heavy but small in size, so that it would sink rapidly through the depth. Ian and his companion, John Nixon, had fished Abberton many times and on each occasion had returned to their respective workshops to modify or reshape their spinners to get a better sinking rate or action. The final agreed pattern was simple: a blade spinner of the Mepps variety, with an elongated shaft on which was threaded a 1-ounce bullet lead. The addition of a lead up the spinning trace, in the accepted fashion, apparently gave all sorts of trouble, notably a tendency to hang up on underwater snags. A secondary problem, when casting, was that the lure had a habit of tangling back in the line as the weight drew the lighter spinner through the air. We could have resorted to heavier spoon baits but the twirling blade spinner had proved itself as the best fish taker.

Armed with a dozen or so weighted spinners, I set out to fish the reservoir on a cold but bright January day. Meeting the lads at the entrance to the works, I noted that they weren't encumbered by the usual nets and tackle boxes associated with the pike man, but just a rod, gaff and shoulder bag. I soon realized why. A huge dropnet was hanging on a gantry above the balcony that led around the tower, and it bore clear evidence of use!

Casting the lures wasn't difficult as the added weight made them fairly zip through the air – and distance was all important as the lure then had to sink a long way. Short casting meant that the spinner described an arc through the water, finishing up against the tower under the angler's feet.

Within minutes I had lost three spinners to the underwater hazards of the cottages below. I had great difficulty in judging the correct moment to close the bale arm and arrest the sinking bait. Then, because of the amount of line stretch, I had trouble in detecting that the bait had touched something deep below. John Nixon, who had lost many baits here, suggested that I make the cast and then count to sixty, by his reckoning the minimum sinking time.

The fishing became exciting, as with each cast I wondered where the bait was – down a sunken chimney or fluttering up the village High Street! There were a few momentary snatches to the line, which I attributed perhaps to bushes or treetop debris. Then John had a solid pull and yanked his rod up into an exaggerated strike. He wound line like mad, for the depth was such that line stretch was difficult to overcome and a fish couldn't be felt until most of the stretch had been taken up. This one played dourly, convincing John that it was neither large nor a pike.

After a few minutes' progressive pumping and winding, a nice perch flapped on to the surface and splashed around while the dropnet was lowered. I don't like that type of net or approve its use, since good fish are liable to be lost even if the angler's companions handle it skilfully. But Gillespie made no mistake, urging John to lead the fish carefully over the net rim sunk a few inches below the water. A positive heave and the fish was on its way up the brickwork.

We continued to spin away but nothing happened for a long time. Fishing a normal bank situation, I would have been tempted to wander off to other water; but the lads insisted that we must stay the course as they knew the pitch and the behaviour of the pike. Evidently the fishing always followed a pattern; very few takes for the first hours, but then the pike would gradually awaken as they saw more and more lures fluttering over their heads. Ian and John had the theory that the pike rested in ambush positions among the buildings below and were not easily aroused since they could at any time take advantage of the vast quantities of shoal fish that provided their daily bread. Because in 90 feet of water there could not be much light, and since the bottom was probably composed of thick Essex mud and silt, the lads had shrewdly reasoned that a lure which flashed in the murky gloom and gave off vibrations from the twirling blade ought to produce more taking fish.

I waited about an hour or more before the first action began. A slight tweak to the line signalled the arrival of a fish as my lure was being wound through the middle level of water. It was the softest of pulls, hardly more than the effect felt when a bait brushes against underwater reeds; but as stretch in the line was taken up, the weight of the fish became apparent.

My rod bowed over and I began to pump the fish. It was not unlike sea angling, where the depth of water made the fishing a straight 'up and down' affair. Occasionally the fish brought my rod down in an increased arc as it stopped in the water, perhaps due to a pressure change effect; all went solid for a minute before the fish began to move again. There was no way that I could speed its rise to the surface. It came steadily and progressively, without any frantic escape movements. Only when I judged the fish to be almost at the surface did anything start to happen. The dour tug of war ended and a huge head broke the surface about 30 feet out. Then the fish began to move away from the base of the tower. I had to give line as the slipping drag sang.

Because of the balcony's height above reservoir level, I could now see that it was a big pike of maybe 20 lbs. I looked around for my companions, and got a nasty shock. I was alone on the tower. I hadn't noticed them disappear, being too busy with my unaccustomed type of spinner. My predicament was obvious. I had to beat the fish and then struggle with the dropnet!

Luckily, I did the right thing. Keeping the fish on a tight line well away from the tower, I swung the gantry out from the wall with my left hand. There were a few heart-stopping moments as I fought to keep control of the fish and to release the rope from its cleat. Finally, as the rope ran through the pulley, the net began to drop. I glanced quickly over the railings to see that the net rim was well below the surface and then tied a hitch in the rope.

My pike was swimming in an arc, tethered by the line, threatening to vanish behind the tower, where a walkway ran back to the concrete banking. I had to prevent this because the supporting framework of the walkway disappeared into the water, and a big fish could easily run the nylon against the metal uprights and get away. I put tension on the rod to halt the pike in its tracks and got another scare as it dipped its head and thrashed a huge tail in a sequence of sweeps that lifted a spray from the surface.

Slowly, very slowly, the fish began to move toward me. I kept the line tight as it moved, head-shaking, through the surface film. I was shaking too but the fish was tiring. It started to roll over on to its side where I could clearly see the bait, jammed into the fleshy corner of the lower jaw. Closer in, the fish took on frightening proportions, its weight growing, in my mind, as I inched it toward the security of the sunken net.

Not everything goes to plan when fishing – and this was one of those times! I led the fish to the net and it promptly swam straight through the three cords that spanned the net rim. With a fish the wrong side of the net and the nylon only 10 lb, I could have done with some help. Since I couldn't clear the line from the dropnet, it became a matter of gently lifting the rod tip to bring the fish back. Fortunately it worked.

Probably because of a pressure change effect, the fish allowed me to bring it in, back toward the net. As the head crossed the rim and then the body, I gave a heave and the net was clear of the water. I rested for an instant, put the rod down and began to haul. The pike lost nothing in size as it came up; it was my largest ever, but what made it really special was the way it was taken and the mysterious environment from which it came.

I had removed the hooks by the time my companions came back but they helped with weighing and photographs. Then John asked if he could have the fish. I didn't need it and pike preservation was not high on the list of angling priorities then; so it was despatched humanely and loaded into John's car.

My pike from Abberton Reservoir, not huge but satisfying because of the unique environment in which it lived. There must be many far bigger pike in the lowland reservoirs.

A couple of weeks later I heard what had happened to my prize catch. John had shown it to his family and friends. It was 24½ lbs and aroused quite an interest. But John had a predicament. What to do with a big pike that begins to give off an unpleasant odour? A solution came to him in a flash. On the way to work he passed a famous Surrey fishery. What better than return the fish to a water where it would become part of the continuing food chain? So in went the pike and John forgot about it.

A week later a piece in a local paper headlined that two youngsters had caught a monster pike, which appeared to have gone on growing after death – it was stated to have weighed over 25 lbs! One angling newspaper and a national Sunday followed up with stories and, I believe, prizes to mark the achievement. And to this day there is a tackle shop in Surrey which has the fish set up for all to see – clearly a case of opportunism all round!

CHAPTER NINE

Tale of a Working Man

GIBRALTAR

You know how it is in any harbour. Men working down in a boat, as she gently rubs her fenders against the quay wall, are of great public interest! Now and then you look up to see what is happening, who is taking an interest in your efforts to maintain the engine, pump the bilges or scrub the decks.

I was enjoying a week's fishing with Les Moncrieff, in Gibraltar, during the 1966 European Sea Angling Championships. We had borrowed a nice little sea boat to fish around in the Straits while the rest of the visiting fishermen were striving to win trophies and the like. Every morning it was our welcome chore to ensure the filters were clean and the bearings greased before we left harbour to find and fish a seabed that was new to us both.

Peering up and along the harbour wall, my gaze lingered on what was so obviously an English couple. Elderly, they were dressed in a style that took me back to my days in the Far East. Neither spoke, but were completely engrossed in what Les and I were doing. After ten minutes our viewers were still standing above us, so I invited them aboard to take a look around the craft. They climbed gingerly down the harbour steps and into the boat.

After a few questions and answers had been exchanged about origins, Les brought out the charts to explain where we fished, for what and, with a little difficulty, why! They proved to be a delightful pair so I asked if they might like to join us for a day's fishing. The old lady shook her head sadly, saying that she had never been to sea and didn't think that it was for her. However, her man responded eagerly, explaining that he had always wanted to go out in a small boat but never had found the time.

We arranged to pick up the old chap, on the following morning, at the Rock Hotel. Now that is one place where only the rich can afford to stay.

Early next day we roared up to the hotel in an incredibly small and battered taxi, to find our shipmate already waiting on the steps in the warm sun. I shall call him Tom because he looked like a sound man, and had a Yorkshire bluffness, accompanied by plain speaking, that admirably suited him and his home county.

Tom was handed into the car by a porter who then asked us if he could put a picnic basket in the boot. I thought he meant something fairly small and wasn't quite expecting the enormous hamper that another chap staggered out

What a lucky chap . . . he has the right girlfriend. One who will muck in, squeezing sardines pounded with bran to make the rubby-dubby for a day's sharking off Gibraltar!

with from the hotel. Little was said as we negotiated Main Street, on the way to the harbour, for this was rather like trying to drive a London bus through a Calcutta bazaar!

At the harbour we unfolded ourselves from the taxi to embark our gear – and the hamper – on board. As Les readied the boat, I asked Tom what he would like to do or see. He replied that any plans of ours would be fine with him. He seemed slightly bemused by all the noise and gaiety of the harbour where the competitors in the festival were piling tackle and themselves aboard the many charter boats, and was perhaps just content to lean back and soak up the atmosphere.

After checking that we were fit to move, I started the engine and shouted back to Tom that today we were going to Africa. Now that really shifted him. Open-mouthed, he leapt up from his seat in the well. 'Africa,' he almost shrieked, 'I don't think that my wife would like to have me away that long!'

Pointing seaward to where a grey smudge sat low on the horizon, I quietly told him that Africa lay just across the Straits, not more than an hour or so away. Clearly our companion of the day had no idea about the geography of the Mediterranean. As we let our ropes go and started away from the crowded quay, his face lit up, like a child who had been given a special toy.

While we cruised on a sparkling sea, flat and calm, Les talked to Tom about Morocco and the coast close to Ceuta, where we intended to fish the deepwater for grouper. He asked a hundred questions, but not the usual trivia that sea anglers are subjected to by people who watch our antics in harbour. Tom wanted to know about the sea, the navigation and the reasons we were sportfishermen. 'Why don't you sell the fish you catch?' That was a bit difficult to answer. 'It's because we are amateurs,' was a reply that didn't quite seem to satisfy him. 'Can you be sure to catch a grouper?' he asked. 'Well,' I mumbled, 'it's a matter of identifying the kind of seabed where groupers live. Then we have to simulate the sort of bait that they feed on and present it so that it looks truly alive. If we get those things right, there's more than a chance that we can hook a grouper, or stone bass as they are more often called.' I could see we were likely to be in an embarrassing position if we didn't get to grips with some sort of sizeable fish. Without boasting, we implied that we were quietly confident and would have no problem in bringing home a grouper. To explain that large specimens are thin on the ground and need to be worked hard for was left unsaid.

Our charts, backed up by the sound knowledge of fishing friends from Gibraltar, suggested that we drift over a patch of reef comprising a sort of undersea cliff seabed where a ledge rising 3–4 fathoms from the bottom gave perfect grouper habitat. The grouper feeds by ambushing shoals of small fish that swim along the face of reefs and such underwater situations as offer caves or crevices to the predator. While I had conned the boat, Les had been busy making his own system of rigs and mounting the baits.

Grouper can grow to enormous sizes. I had seen fish of over 100 lbs in the fish market, so the rigs were made up of three strands of 50-lb nylon plaited together, each strand terminating in an 8/0 forged hook. On each hook Les had mounted three sardines which, when hung over the side, looked remarkably like a small shoal of live fish. We thought that our best chance was to fish them with a 'sink and draw' action.

I had to keep my promise of going across the Straits, but the voyage turned out not to be as productive as I had imagined. We found a super reef a half mile or so off the low, sandy coast, lowered the baits but got nothing resembling a bite from fish. The water was far too clear, with visibility many fathoms to the bottom. After an hour trying everything, we cut our losses to head back in to Gibraltar waters. Even now I have a funny feeling that the reef on which we decided to try our luck might have been just inside Spanish territorial waters, which, at that time, could have created an international incident!

The mark, nominated by our Gibraltarian sea anglers, turned out to be located in 29 fathoms of water. At first the drift wasn't perfect, as what breeze there was took us diagonally across the bulk of the reef. Les talked me into a dummy run so that he could test his way across the rock deep below us, raising and lowering his unbaited tackle to the variation in depth and obstruction. Satisfied, he shouted that we could motor upwind for the first of our serious drifts.

We made two long, slow drifts before anything happened, though neither of us got hooked into the foul ground below – something that usually happens when the seabed is right for big fish. Meanwhile, Tom took an avid interest in all that was happening, in fact his encouragement kept us working away lifting and repeatedly dropping our baits back to contact the seabed.

It wouldn't be true to say I felt an actual bite. What happened came as one hell of a shock. Something grabbed the baits and I was yanked sharply forward across the gunwale, with a fearful thump on the ribs. Before I even had time to wonder whether I had cracked them or not, my rod tip went below the surface. It went down and stayed down. Line jerked off the spool, against the clutch, while I could do nothing but hang on!

At first I thought that the speed of drift had caught me unaware. I felt as though the sinker or hooks, or both, were fast in the reef. But then the reef seemed to *move* – to begin a powerful jagging action, as though a great fish was shaking its head to throw off its tether.

I can't say that I played the fish for the first five minutes – it played me. I was totally breathless and could manage little effort after hitting the side of the boat. With my line as taut as a bowstring, I looked to Les for advice. He was rapidly winding in his gear, which took some time, but urged me to 'hang in there and get some lift into the rod'.

More easily said than done! I couldn't get the fish moving at all. Each time I began to pump, the fish would respond by yanking the rod over hard. I had a slight difficulty, too, with the height of the gunwale; there was rather more freeboard than was really necessary for a seaworthy boat. Pumping properly requires that the rod can be brought up from just above the horizontal and that was something I couldn't manage. Things improved, however, as the boat continued its drift. There was a noticeable change in line angle which, combined with the gradual tightening of my nylon, began to give me an edge on the fish. Situations like these make one realize that 50-lb line and the inherent power in a good rod blank can take a hell of a battering!

After another five minutes of virtual stalemate, there was a sudden movement from the fish, which embarked on what seemed to be a series of short runs. One can only surmise what actually happens below the waves, but on reflection I think that the grouper had tired of trying to get back to a particular spot on the reef and was veering sideways in search of a place that offered darkness. Even at that depth there must have been quite a lot of light filtering through to produce conditions that the fish didn't know or like.

It took me a further ten minutes before I felt that the fish was being controlled. By then I could pump, getting some line back, and only spasmodic flashes of sudden movement came back up the nylon. Then I knew that the fish was mine. . . .

Les leapt around the boat, peering over the sides for a first glimpse of the fish. Tom may not have understood exactly what was going on, but he must have realized that the excitement heralded something special. Another

Les Moncrieff with my grouper (or Cherna or stone bass), which weighed 58½ lbs. It was a lion of a fish – with a mouth large enough to swallow a football!

minute or so and we could see the fish as it rose through the water. Chocolate-brown in colour, massive and with a mouth like Blackwall Tunnel, the grouper broke the surface film to lie, flapping its fins, in the sunlight!

Moncrieff doesn't miss with a gaff. One sweep and he had the fish securely held. I dropped the rod and we both hauled my first ever grouper over the high gunwale. It hit the deck and I sank on to a side-thwart, gasping, only able to stare at the fish while my muscles began to tremble. I didn't know whether to laugh or cry. Bringing aboard such a magnificent deepwater specimen was an experience to be savoured.

We didn't hang around on the mark. It was back to Gib for a welcome rest, although there wasn't much talking done en route, for the contents of Tom's hamper had to be consumed. We had temporarily forgotten all about his bottles of wine and appetizing salads on real china plates, but now we had the time to belt into the goodies! Gib's local television station wanted to hear all about the fight, and since Les went along for the interview, they naturally credited him with the capture! I didn't mind, for I knew that without Leslie's strength and the angling knowledge of our Gibraltarian friends, I could never have brought such a fish ashore.

That evening we were invited up to the Rock Hotel by our new friends. Amid pleasant conversation, and their profuse thanks, it emerged that dear old Tom and his good lady were taking their very first holiday. Together, back in industrial Yorkshire, they had worked to build a business and raise a family, never having found enough time to get away on their own. Even now, twenty years on, I can remember the genuine pleasure that shone from their faces and the pride in having helped to capture the grouper.

'Why don't you post it home?'

While the competitors in the European Championship were battling it out for national supremacy, Les and I took ourselves off to fish the rough ground beyond Europa Point, the sharp bit of Gibraltar that juts out into the Straits. The seabed was composed of huge lumps of broken rock – a favoured habitat for huge sea bream. It was hard to identify some of the fish we took over the foul ground. The local names, 'pargo' and 'sargo', meant little to us, as there are so many sea bream species in the Mediterranean Sea and too few accurate identification booklets available for visiting anglers.

We had a lot of fun and a deal of fish but it wasn't to be bream that made our day. No, we were to tangle with a much larger, more ungainly fellow. Les was fishing away, on what he and I both thought was a patch of extremely rough seabed, when he experienced a soft pull. He didn't strike at once, muttering in excitement that the bite could be from yet another grouper quietly mouthing a rather large lash of fishbait. So he gave the fish time to take a firm hold and then struck.

A sunfish comes to our boat off Europa Point. There is little fight from
the species, just a solid weight that exerts tremendous pressure on both
the rod and the angler.

The line sang with its stretch, yet there was no reaction at all from whatever
was below the boat. 'Feels like a sickly skate – there's no fight in it!' he yelled.
There was another angling craft within hailing distance and the occupants
were taking a lively interest in the fight. Someone shouted, 'You can do better
than that, put your back into it!' which evidently so riled Les that he produced
a superhuman effort.

'Mike,' he gasped. 'Whatever I've got on is rolling itself up in the line.
Could be a shark.' I agreed with him, for we had often had similar behaviour
at home from both porgies and blue sharks, which would spin in the water,
rolling their bodies up the nylon. It can spell danger for both angler and shark.
The line may be cut, and the shark, struggling to break free, can die because its
swimming movement, and thus its breathing, is impeded.

The pressure applied by Moncrieff gradually told on the fish, and he was
able to recover line steadily. It took a very long time before either of us got a
glimpse of the fish. Then, about 20 feet below the boat a grey, round object

emerged from the gloom. It rose with a circling, oscillating motion, rather like a coin dropped into water that seesaws as it falls. To our astonishment, Les had a sunfish (*Mola mola*) on his hook! The books will tell you that sunfish are plankton feeders, inhabiting the upper, warm water layers of the ocean. Well, here was one that liked to eat large lashes of bait, especially when they were on the bottom in 30 fathoms!

We laughed uproariously when we saw what that sunfish had done to the line. Nylon was wrapped around it so many times that the fish looked like a badly tied Christmas parcel. Sure enough, one of the spectators in the adjacent boat guffawed, 'Why don't you stick a stamp on it, then you can post it home?' Very funny, I thought, but Les had the perfect reply: 'What – at the weight that I catch 'em? You've got to be joking!'

The ocean sunfish is a spectacular beast, ungainly but interesting. Most books about fish identification describe it as a drab grey in colour . . . which couldn't be further from the truth!

CHAPTER TEN

Halibut, Huge Skate and Hoy

ORKNEY ISLANDS

The Norsemen were certainly tough characters! They had to be, if only to fend off the lashing rain and biting Atlantic wind that hit me as I arrived in this northerly outpost of the British Isles. The fishing plan, worked out in the peace of Leslie Moncrieff's parlour in Surrey, was simple in theory but, as it turned out, rather more difficult to execute.

The idea was to make a documentary film in the Orkneys about catching really big fish. We wanted a halibut, newly regarded as the acme for sea anglers, and, for comparative purposes, a skate which, at that time, would

The windswept Orkney Islands, looking out from Stromness to the Atlantic Ocean. They are the home of halibut and huge common skate, with the security of Scapa Flow providing a variety of marks.

represent a rod and line 'first' for the islands. The film crew were all anglers (a blessing when work starts and technical jargon has to be translated into instant thought and action), while Julian Strange, our producer, had been among the Rank school of actors and could be guaranteed to cut a confident figure in front of the camera, quite apart from dragging the production together when the crunch came.

Michael Shepley was to join us from Edinburgh. Although still a university student there, he was emerging as one of Scotland's talked-about sea anglers. He already had experience of fishing in Orkney waters and for a long time held the Scottish conger record.

We flew to Kirkwall, as I remember, in a Viscount, low enough in those days to glimpse something of Scotland below, the Grampian mountains, the miles of lonely beaches and sea cliffs that ached for the presence of a rod and, finally, the majestic Pentland Firth. Now, as then, the place makes me shiver. When tossed by storms, this watery division between Scotland's mainland and the Earldom of the Orkneys takes on a viciousness that hurls massive seas on to the rocky shores, hammering the cliffs into subjection. Weird granite projections and deeply carved sea-caves abound along the islands' Atlantic coast, suggesting that these treeless, grass-topped rocky lands are 'standing in the way' of the ocean's windswept power.

Clearly we would need capable guides in these restless seas, and Michael had organized two such men from the town of Stromness. George and Frank Sinclair had spent most of their lives tending lobster creels under the cliffs. They knew all about storms and the heavy cost to be paid when pots were laid in the face of an Atlantic blow. Judging the weather signs and deciding to sail or stay within the confines of the tiny harbour were part and parcel of their daily lives.

We crept from our warm beds, breakfasted and lurched on to the quay in the early morn. The Sinclairs' boat was very small but eminently suitable for the tenuous occupation of potting the reefs and rocky gullies under the Cliffs of Hoy. As the skipper pointed out, 'A smallish craft keeps paying a profit in the hard times, and she's safe in under the rocks.' My concern was less for his profit than for my precarious filming perch! I could lash the camera and its tripod on to the tiny wheelhouse roof but I didn't fancy having to sway around, behind the film gear, with an eye glued to the viewfinder. Another annoying thing was that my position on the wheelhouse was too far away from the scene of the fishing action for me to creep down and indulge in a bit of sport myself.

Anyway, the sea was calming as we sailed on our first day's fishing to an area within Stromness Sound. At Leslie's request, George agreed to anchor up to the edge of a tide rip. Les's experience in Ireland with large common skate and a beautiful halibut from off the Kerry coast had persuaded him that both species tended to hover along the line where fast, tidal water 'rubbed' along the edge of standing water. He reckoned that resident shoal species, like pollack, used the swirling eddies created by the faster water to ambush weaker-swimming fish which had trouble combating the currents. We had reason to believe that pollack, as a hookbait, had tempted halibut to strike in previous encounters, although information was sketchy. To the best of our knowledge, only two halibut had been taken on rod and line in Britain in recent years. Bunt Knight, the provost of Stromness, had landed one fish and James Scott had followed up with another a few months before our arrival.

As a result, all the talk now, among angling journalists and pot hunters alike, was about halibut. Most of the written stuff was rubbish, based on theories expounded in books dating from the 1920s and 1930s. The fact was that nobody had the least idea of what to expect from this giant flatfish – nobody apart from our two Orkney veterans who gave us straightforward accounts based on first-hand experience.

Half an hour's boat ride and we were anchored within a few hundred yards of the eastward, sloping side of Hoy. Away from the full force of the Atlantic westerlies, the land was softer, greener and grazed by the stout-legged cattle for which the islands are famous. We had pollack for baits plus a few frozen mackerel thoughtfully provided by George. The tackles were simple, stout rods of about 50-lb class with the appropriate nylon lines. The terminal rigs were of 150-lb BS cable-laid wire, a necessary precaution for both skate and halibut; the grinding teeth of the former and the sharp teeth of the latter are both capable of cutting through nylon like butter when the line is under tension.

Since Julian and I had agreed that work was to come first, only Mike and Leslie had serious rigs over the boat's side. It was a good decision because within ten minutes Leslie had his first reaction from the seabed. It started as a rapid series of nodding movements to the rod tip, and then a traditional plonking pull that yanked the tip over in an arc. We had been warned that various members of the ray family could well be attracted to the hookbaits, so Les was somewhat lethargic in reacting to the bite. Just as well, for by the time he decided that something really was taking an interest, the fish was well and truly on. There was no question of striking. Just lifting the rod was enough to convince him the line was under pressure, and such pressure could not be applied by one of the smaller rays!

Conditions inside the Sound were ideal for playing a big fish. Although a strongish sea was still running outside the islands, we sat in relatively mirror-like conditions. Only a riffle of wind had any effect, barely enough to break the smooth surface of the sea loch. Les Moncrieff was, and is, a big man, yet the first pressure he applied caused him to take an involuntary step aft toward the boat's gunwale, indicating just how big his fish was.

Tradition dictates that whenever somebody hooks into a sizeable fish, the other anglers bring in their lines. That rule is particularly important when attempting to film the effort. Inevitably, people get into shot and have to be yelled at to clear the camera's viewpoint. Otherwise there may be chaos and heartache later in the cutting room when a distorted head appears in the frame and ruins what might have been an exciting sequence. My screams, and Julian's blunt language had the desired effect, so Les was able to get into playing his fish with the camera on him and the arcing rod.

Skate don't come easy; in fact, they have always been the species to cause me most trouble! When a large fish keeps using its fins, part of the strain is removed from the angler's back by a constant change in fishing direction. Skate hang in the tide, lying with little movement but a movement that has to be held, or the fish dives. I have never really been able to take that kind of constant back strain that starts with a dull ache and ends by convincing you that your legs are going to give way.

Moncrieff handled the skate purposefully, letting it move ponderously off down the slow-flowing tide, then applying enough rod pressure to turn the fish so that it swam toward the boat and rose a little in the water. His worries came when the skate surfaced about 40 yards behind the anchored boat and lay finning on the surface. The tide pulled in one direction and Leslie in the other, but he won, gradually working the huge, beaten fish back to the transom.

Julian waited with the gaff, which was a bit special. Leslie, the eternal optimist, had long since acquired a 'Zane Grey' big-game gaff with a detachable head and rope, extremely useful when shark fishing or trying to secure huge sea fish that are never really caught until they are in the boat. The gaff went home and we had our first Orkney skate flapping hard on the boat's floorboards.

It was a female fish of around 120 lbs. The old saying has it that where there is a female, you will find a male, so over went the baited rigs again, and in almost no time Mike Shepley's rod tip was nodding. This fish gave almost a repeat performance of the first fight. We reasoned that as the water was fairly shallow, only about 8 fathoms, the fish would make longer runs away from the boat, and so it proved. The gentler line angle made for a slightly easier fight. Had the line been straight up and down, the struggle would have bent the angler's back but, as it was, he was able to exert the full power of his shoulders. Mike swore that the fish was stronger and heavier than Leslie's, and our first sight of it certainly gave the impression of greater size. Instead of sliding back across the tide to the boat, each time Mike recovered a few yards of line the fish would flap its wings to drag it off. We thought of dropping the boat back on the anchor rope but were assured by the intrepid angler that he was fully in command.

Julian got a bit bored waiting for the fight to end and, keeping his gear well clear of Mike's, craftily let a bait drop to the seabed, probably hoping for a quick action replay himself. Leslie, meanwhile, was instructing Mike to move

A female common skate from Scapa Flow; she produced a dour fight,
'lying' on the tide, that had Moncrieff sweating as he worked the fish
to the stern against the tide.

back to the wheelhouse, thus further shortening the amount of line out and
getting the angler clear of the transom area for his gaffing activity. The hook
flashed over the side and Mike's skate was neatly taken in the outer margin of
a wing. Julian had to abandon his rod and help Les heave the skate inboard. It
proved indeed to be a male and well over the size of the earlier female.

By now we were experiencing slack water, not the best time for any form of
bottom fishing, though, as Les said, 'Things always come alive as the tide
freshens.' Meanwhile we gutted and cut more bait into hearty lashes. The
offal tossed over the side and the few scraps thrown to hovering gulls soon
attracted the attention of the seabirds. Kittiwakes and fulmars arrived,
swooping and gliding in continuous circles around the boat. Both are fairly
noisy species but the fulmars created a terrible racket as they quarrelled and
fought for scraps. It's strange how gulls and other ocean birds that spend their
lives far out from the shore show little fear of human presence when they pay

their annual visit to the breeding colonies. Either the need for food overrides their natural timidity or they do not associate us with danger.

With the coming of the flood we began fishing seriously once more. The mackerel baits were all used up, so we had to resort to the pollack. The baits demonstrated, almost at once, their pulling power when a couple of dogfish latched on to the offerings. It was an hour or more before the next skate bite was detected, signified on this occasion by a rapid dipping of Julian's rod tip, accompanied by the rattle of the reel's ratchet as line was slowly pulled off the lightly set drag.

As Les and Mike hovered in the background and quietly gave advice, Julian lifted the rod and swept it up in a hefty strike. His 'rod held high' pose was immediately ruined as the power of the skate walloped the rod over into a healthy bend. It ran and ran! Over 50 yards of line disappeared in a half a minute – and there was no sign that the fish intended to stop.

The Sinclairs were dancing about in excitement: three skates for the Orkney Islands and all of them aboard their boat. From my precarious perch on the wheelhouse roof I could only listen to the running commentary and watch the antics of five grown men capering around like schoolboys.

Julian's extended fight with the fish gave me a lot of shooting time and the

Mike's halibut, largest of the flatfish species, is brought across the gunwale. The fish was iced down and flown to London, where it provided dinner in a children's hospital.

Three of the skate caught within the sheltered waters of Scapa Flow,
where the mixed ground of the seabed provides perfect habitat.
Shipwreckage, from the First World War, adds to the tackle hazards.

opportunity to load a much-needed film magazine. After his initial trepidation, he seemed to be handling the skate beautifully, especially from the camera's point of view. An angler sometimes works like mad to get the fish aboard, thinking, quite wrongly, that this will look good on film. Actually, more often than not, the condensed action that such speed entails looks quite unreal to the knowledgeable audience.

We got the third of our big fish aboard and decided that enough was enough. Orkney had its skates . . . and we deserved the hot whiskies that awaited us in the Stromness Hotel. Not that the return to harbour was uneventful. Within minutes of our landfall, the whole town seemed to have got wind of the 'braw fush'! There were willing hands to drag the skate to the scales and to hang them where they could best be seen.

We left the harbour early on the morrow. I was hardly in the best of spirits as I seemed to ache everywhere. Balancing for hours on the wheelhouse had forced me to use muscles not normally employed and they were telling me to slow down! Again the Sinclairs elected to stay within the vast area of semi-protected water that forms the western entrance to Scapa Flow. We only steamed for a few miles beyond our skate territory before they kicked the engine out of gear and started discussing the shore marks.

The ground was right for halibut, a mixture of broken rock which, according to George, ran in lines from the shore with sandy gullies between them.

The tackle was in readiness; Les said that exactly the same gear was correct but he wanted a slightly longer wired trace, reckoning that about a fathom would give a bait that extra freedom to wash around in the slightly stronger tidal flow. Halibut are demersal fish but they will move up in the water to ambush other species and are extremely fast movers. While we waited, with the rods leaned on the gunwale, the wind began to blow, making the sea a bit choppy. My camera gear was already lashed in its former position, but for the time being I preferred to remain in the warmth of the wheelhouse chatting to our boatmen. Meanwhile Mike and Les both had a succession of fish, mostly dogs, with the occasional pollack coming as a freshly baited hook was lowered.

We waited four hours before Mike got the first bite that suggested a halibut. The fish picked up the bait that was lying hard on the seabed and began to move, accompanied by a steady clicking from the multiplier. Mike flicked the ratchet off and let the movement build up into a positive run. We all assumed it was skate until the drag was tightened; then we saw a definite nodding action to the rod tip, inconsistent with the flapping motion of a skate. This run was much quicker!

Mike's strike was firm and it stopped the fish momentarily; then the fun started. As I scrambled for the camera, I caught a glimpse of Shepley sinking to his knees. 'Funny time to start praying,' flashed through my mind. But it was simply that the fish had other ideas about being halted in mid-flight. It took line at a hell of a speed and then seemed to slow, perhaps having come across a rocky outcrop. The fight now took on a different pattern. Mike gained some line with vigorous pumping, and then it was all lost in a few seconds as the fish yanked the rod over again. Mike's a big lad, not quite Leslie Moncrieff's stamp, but well able to exert a tremendous pressure when he feels the need. However, here was something not easily overcome. Furthermore, the pattern of the fish's fight, as we saw it transmitted up the line to the telling rod tip, differed vastly from previous experience with other large species. Only Les had ever landed a halibut before and he kept muttering, 'Got to be. . . . Got to be,' as the battle progressed. He explained that the bouncing of the rod tip was caused by the fish's tail striking the line as it bore down. Several times, from my high vantage point, I thought that I could see a flash in the water. Then I did get a true glimpse of a white diamond shape in the water below. The fish went under the boat and circled around a couple of times before anybody else got a sight of it.

George was holding the gaff ready, with explicit instructions from Leslie to make certain that the fish was gaffed in the head. Anywhere else could be disastrous as the halibut was known to exert a last-minute power that could tear the gaff right out through the flesh of its thickset body. The rope was tied around a cleat and the gaff extended over the side. Mike was sweating buckets as the fish swept around and up to the surface. In went the gaffhook, slightly behind the gillcase, but it took a perfect hold. We had our first halibut in the boat and Mike's grin was a sight to behold!

By mutual agreement, we called it a day and motored back to town. We had the satisfaction of knowing that our fish wasn't to be wasted. Jo Grimond, the island's MP, had arranged in advance with BEA that what we caught would be flown down to London to a children's hospital. All in all, it had been a rewarding expedition, even though, for a change, I had played a somewhat passive role.

Our constant companions at sea – fulmars *Fulmarus glacialis*.

CHAPTER ELEVEN

Wrecks and Conger Eels

ENGLAND

Clicking to a rhythmic pattern, the Decca numbers indicated the track of *Our Unity* as she ploughed across the swells on a southerly course out from Brixham. Consulting his pocketbook, a written record of Decca Navigator numbers for all the known wrecks that lie in Torbay, John Trust gave an imperceptible nod to Ernie Passmore, his partner and co-skipper of the most famous of British sea-angling boats. Passmore busied himself with a tangle of ropes, polythene bottles and a dahn buoy. The boat slowed, made a turn uptide and the whole caboodle was hurled over the gunwale.

Unity continued to motor slowly on her course as John referred constantly both to the Decca and the graph sounder that lay alongside on the wheel-house shelf. Gradually he backed off the engine revolutions, peering astern to where the dahn buoy had settled on the lazy swell. Only five of the eight polythene bottles were showing above the surface. John muttered to me, above the rumbling engine, that the number of visible bottles indicated the strength of the running tidestream. The bottle floats also told him the distance that the anchor had to be set, uptide, so that the anchored boat could drop back to lie perfectly placed at the uptide side of the wreck. In 40 fathoms of water the calculation seemed to me to be very much a 'rule of thumb' operation; but I had immediate proof of the ability of these two men when the wreck appeared on the echo-sounder graph paper as cable was released from the winch amidships. Neither John nor Ernie were happy with the first positioning, so they wound in enough cable to clear the anchor and motored *Unity* upstream again. Then came a positive anchoring which brought smiles from everyone.

Wreck fishing is all about the placing of the fishing vessel relative to the wreck below on the seabed. Tide stream, surface wind direction and depth of water all have to be taken into account. We had motored out for almost three hours to find the mark that John told us was a 'virgin' wreck, never before fished by sea anglers. The Decca numbers in the pocketbook, which he guarded so jealously, were presents from unfortunate trawler skippers who had hung their trawlnets up on the wreckage during their commercial activities. So we anglers were to benefit from the misfortune of others!

While my companions, all guests of Hardy Brothers, frantically set about forming the necessary terminal rigs to handle this gruelling fishing, I talked to the skippers. I wanted to know about the wreck below us and the development of such accurate navigation that was vital to pinpointing it. John Trust was loth to show me his book or its numbers, but what they did reveal helped me to understand the success of these stout men of Devon.

They had literally hundreds of logged wreck positions, with many of the hulks named and given an accurate size, 'one for every day of the year,' said John, laconically. Most of the wrecks in the Torbay areas were the result of wartime sinkings, as the convoys made the Western Approaches. Now they had become seabed larders, providing huge havens of security to a variety of fish species that offer something special in rod and line fishing. Commercial boats may trawl alongside the thickly populated wrecks but can never seriously reduce the fish numbers without the risk to themselves of losing expensive gear.

The fishing on that day was in the nature of a proving session. Hardy, and their adviser on rod design, Leslie Moncrieff, were anxious to put their new 'Saltwater' range of rods to the ultimate test and, at the same time, try to create a new wreck fishing catch record. So, we had all been given identical rods with Penn 6/o reels loaded with 50-lb nylon to which we added a simple single-hook, wired leger rig. The bait was fresh mackerel, unsurpassed as the best lure for all bottom fish.

Letting the baits down carefully, to prevent tangles, seemed to take ages, punctuated now and then by cries of 'I'm in the wreck' or 'Soft bottom, must have dropped on the sand', from excited members of the boat's company. I find the ideal bait position is into the scour, that gully formed by the action of seabed currents as they sweep around the ends of the wreck, and which always holds eels. I am supported in this opinion by Royal Navy divers who assure me that the scour is always present on the side of the wreck opposite to that subjected to the more powerful phase of tide, and that the gouged-out scour is full of congers! Further away from the wreck, sand builds up in banks that make an ideal habitat for turbot and other bottom-feeding species which like open ground. Over the top of a wreck, among masts or other tangles, the open water is populated by smaller fish which fall prey to the marauding cod, pollack and other powerful swimmers that visit the scene.

Skippers who spend a lot of time at sea on congering forays maintain that one must first go for and remove the smaller conger eels before fish of any real size get a chance to take the baits. Possibly the smaller eels get among the baits because of their swimming speed, the larger, resident specimens having to move out from their homes in innumerable cracks and crevices that are ideal places of ambush for a meal. Our first day's fishing started off in the

Anglers concentrate on their fishing while John Trust removes the trace
from a small conger. He found that trace removal was best left for a
while, certainly until the agitated fish quietened.

prescribed fashion – numerous strap eels that immediately grabbed the baits
as soon as they hit the seabed.

It was a long way down to the bottom and seemed even longer when
winding up a small eel. Everybody got into congers, occasionally producing a
better fish that weighed about 40 lbs or so. Sometimes the baits didn't reach
the seabed, for they were intercepted, over the wreck's superstructure, by a
pollack, cod or sinuous ling. These fish were a very acceptable bonus to the
catch of eels, which none of us could visualize ending in a frying pan!

As the day wore on, our catch grew steadily and the congers got slightly
larger. The changing tide brought fishing to a stop as *Unity* swung away from
the lie of the wreck to put our baited hooks on clean sand, a move that failed to

produce a single fish. Ernie suggested that we bury our heads in the lunch boxes, while the boat was motored round to settle the anchor in a new position. This involved the crew hauling in on the cable, lifting the anchor out of the sand and motoring in the opposite direction. Our skippers had a couple of tries before they were completely happy with the way she settled to the new lie. All their efforts were applied to getting our hookbaits down into the scour for the rest of the session.

Early afternoon saw us again pulling congers. The fish seemed larger and we wondered if they had, in their turn, moved around the wreck to take advantage of the direction of tideflow and the possible food that would be swept to them as the current strengthened. John, in his purposeful manner, informed us that we were fishing the small stuff out to clear the decks for tomorrow. Nobody argued, for his experience, accumulated over countless conger fishing trips, mattered if we were to get among the big fish or take any sort of record into the port of Brixham.

I believe we finished the day's angling with 1000 lbs of mixed fish, which for six anglers, feeling their way into the methods of wrecking in deepwater, wasn't bad at all! A number of things had emerged during the actual fishing. We found that our wire traces were best left attached to the congers until either of the skippers could find time to extract the hook from the fish. It is no fun, and decidedly dangerous, to extract a hook from the mouth of a conger that twists and slithers along the deck as you fight to restrain it. So each of us had made up a batch of hook traces with quick-release loops. We also realized that it was imperative to keep the deck free of all tackle and possessions not involved in the fishing. Too much time was spent avoiding tackle boxes and repositioning the spare gear with which we had all cluttered ourselves.

I found that the first ten or so yards of reel line, next to the swivel and sliding sinker boom, was being constantly frayed. Although we were all aware of the sharp edges on a sunken ship's plates and scattered wreckage, we didn't feel a lot of line rubbing at those depths. Presumably the line can be drawn into a mass of rubbish by taking fish, while the inherent line stretch, in nylon, absorbs much of the fish's movement, markedly reducing the sensitivity at the rod tip.

The use of braided line would give a much improved indication of a bite and subsequent fish movement, but braided material is far more prone to parting after abrasion. I found that a lash of mackerel that covered the hook point and shank was far less likely to get fast in wreckage than a sliver that left the point bare. I started by tying on the lashes of bait but soon lost interest in making it totally secure when I realized that few baits were actually torn off from the iron. Obviously these eels were far too greedy to become hook shy.

When we arrived back in Brixham's inner harbour we were met by a crowd of holidaymakers and a lorry from the fish market. The latter was a good sign as it meant that nothing of the catch would be wasted – a charge that has often

Evening return to Brixham harbour after our first day's fishing over the
Torbay wrecks was an exciting time, the crowds of holidaymakers
making wild guesses as to the weight of each fish.

been levelled at boat fishermen. Too many catches of conger have been dumped unceremoniously into the harbour once the 'Great White Hunter' pictures are taken.

Next morning came with another calm sea and cloudless sky. Our three hours' sailing passed quickly as gear was 'polished', and bait carefully filleted, while Ernie battered our ears with his 'Orders of the Day'. John Trust put the craft over the wreck, the sounder trace showing exactly the same towering, seabed shapes that I had witnessed on the previous day's positioning. The tide was slightly stronger, as we had the advantage of an additional hour's fall to full ebb. Our baits streamed over the gunwales and we all hit bottom together. Fish started pulling at the baits immediately. Five out of six rods buckled to the pull of fish, while the remaining hookbait went straight into a tangle of wreckage – and stuck there! It was mine and I felt sick as I fought to break out from the holdfast. Ten minutes work saw me dropping down a new baited trace, as I thought, into the scour. Obviously it hadn't quite hit the mark because I immediately felt a sucking bite accompanied by trembling movements of the rod tip as the fish moved off, many fathoms below. I struck and the rod lumped over into something that made no attempt to speed back to the wreck or produce any real fight; it just hung in the tide. John, shrewd observer of all that was happening, muttered 'turbot', as he leaned against the wheelhouse door. 'You're fishing lighter than the others; I'll bet that the lead is out on the sand,' he said. I hadn't intended using a smaller weight to get away from the wreck: it had simply been a question of trying to match the tide and fish with a weight that was sensitive and comfortable to handle.

Ten minutes and a lot of pumping eventually brought my first wreck turbot to the landing net. A fish of 18 lbs, it had 'kited' up in the tide, requiring only a steady line pressure to skate it back to the boat's stern. The fight from this valuable species can be so much more satisfying when fishing in shallower water and with a sinker that doesn't hamper the turbot's effort to break free. Still, it was one fish that wasn't going to see the inside of the fish market!

Although there was a general quickening of interest as my turbot arrived on deck, this soon waned as we were all told bluntly to concentrate on the job in hand – getting through the small straps to the giant congers that we were there to boat. During the first hour there was a noticeable increase in the size of eels that thumped on to the deck of Unity. Les Moncrieff had the first really big specimen, a fish of around 70 lbs. We never knew the accurate weight of any fish while at sea; only the scale in Brixham harbour could be trusted not to exaggerate! Occasionally three or four eels would be on together. With both skippers wielding gaffs, nobody had to wait long for a writhing, surfaced eel to be boated. At times, both John and Ernie had to go into action on one eel, swinging it on both gaffs straight into the stout fish box. There were two of these, with tight fitting lids to prevent eels escaping. They helped to quieten the congers down, the total darkness approximating to seabed conditions.

Shouts of 'Gaff' were more frequent as we all felt the heavier, pulling strains of even bigger fish. The first ferocious tugs always came as the eel was lifted a fathom or so from the seabed. Then I got the impression that contact with the fish only came about as the elasticity in the line was taken up. The conger probably feels its head bent upwards sharply and reacts by trying to spiral down. Most anglers put too much strength into the first part of the fight, but in 40 fathoms that powerful effort is cushioned by the stretching and slackening of the line, produced by the imperceptible rise and fall of the boat on the swell.

When an eel is 4–5 fathoms up, the best of the fight begins. Conger seem to react sharply to the lightening of the water above them, turning down where it is darker and, no doubt in their minds, safer. After the initial flurry of mid-water activity, a big conger comes fairly quietly. Then, as the light penetrates the upper water layers, it catches sight of the boat, at which stage, all hell can break loose! Most sea anglers tend to apply a constant rod pressure until they get a glimpse of the fish rising through the water, and are then tempted to relax as the fish surfaces. Unfortunately, the worst is yet to come. Many marine species can be considered beaten when they arrive alongside the boat, but not the conger, which reserves a last burst of energy for a twisting, spiralling thrash that either pulls the hook free from its jaw or brings the tail crashing across the reel line with a crack that ensures an immediate break. Ernie Passmore's advice to all his anglers is to keep the fish moving slowly from mid-water to the upper layer until a crew member can time his arrival with the gaff, which must coincide with the conger's head broaching the surface film. Then, with a positive but unhurried action, the gaff is driven home and the fish swung aboard in a continuous motion. The expertise of those guys in action was a pleasure to watch.

Apart from a welter of eels, quite a lot of useful panfish came into the boat during the six hours that we fished over that wreck. Cod predominated, though there were plump pollack and one or two superb ling, all of which came from bites detected long before the baits should have hit bottom. The slow drop down evidently encouraged these species to strike at the descending baits. If the bait was lowered fairly fast, it went straight into the scour or wreck, perhaps indicating that the round fish were not actually suspended above the wreck but spent their time patrolling to and fro on a constant search for the unwary. Occasionally, a better than average pouting would be hooked at these depths – and on a 6/o hook loaded with a huge lash of mackerel!

When fishing is good and the skipper hides everything away in the purpose-built fish boxes, anglers can be forgiven for not really being aware of the rate or growth of the catch. We had fished continuously from the time the anchor bit into the bottom until John Trust said that it was time to leave. He left Ernie to the wheel and lifted the covers from the catch boxes. There were gasps from everybody as we gathered around. I wanted photographs on the

High above the wreckage was a shoal of cod which intercepted many
of the baits, intended for conger, as these were lowered through the
mid-water layer.

Peter Collins, a former editor of 'Sea Angler', takes time off to clean the boat as 'Unity' ploughs her way back to Brixham with her decks awash with sinuous eels.

way in to Brixham, and John obligingly spilled everything out on to *Unity*'s roomy stern decking. As fish after fish joined the pile we began to realize the size of our catch. The official weigh-in, after we tied up in Brixham, proved the extent of our achievement. There were 2868 lbs of conger eels, a few hundred pounds of quality panfish and six of the best turbot that I had ever seen! So, some sort of day's record had been set. Although in later years there were to be many larger catches as techniques improved, that Hardy Conger Hunt remains fresh in the memory of every one of us.

CHAPTER TWELVE

Halibut with a Difference

JAPAN

South of industrial Tokyo, in the shadow of the coastal, craggy mountains, lies Atami. Famous for hot springs of some medicinal value, the tiny traditional village is the meeting place of many of the capital city's sea anglers. I had started my fishing experience in the country with a train of visits to rod and reel manufacturing plants but the serious fishing all came about after an introduction to a geisha house!

The men who make Japan's now famous fishing tackle are often accused of not knowing what the gear is really for. So, in an attempt to refute the allegation, they had organized a day's fishing for me on their version of the halibut; but first I was to be treated to a visit to the springs, for a quick cleansing, followed by an introduction to the mystery of Japan's most famous ladies, the geishas. The first shock came when I was joined in the hotel's heated swimming pool by an entire Japanese family, father, mother and their three small, politely smiling daughters. We hadn't one stitch of clothing

Not many of my fishing days have been preceded by such care and attention! I could well have used the geisha's fan in the heat of the following morning's sport.

between us and I was amazed at the genuine freedom that I saw and felt, together with the total lack of prudishness that would have accompanied a similar occurrence in Europe!

Most Europeans have preconceived ideas about the geisha and her function in society. The reality is far different from the wild stories that abound. Tradition is vitally important to the Japanese people and their lives are scrupulously modelled on the values of the past. Geishas are trained from childhood in the almost sacred arts of Japanese music, dance, verse and the ritual tea ceremony. Peace and beauty are the hallmarks of the geisha and the house in which she entertains, and my thoughts were far from the turmoil of sea fishing as I hummed to the haunting melodies played on delicate stringed instruments, the lilt and notes of which defeated me when I tried to remember them later.

Morning saw me out on the hotel balcony, bewitched by the sights and sounds of Atami. Small, apparently top-heavy fishing junks were everywhere, many of them gathered around the periphery of a huge net that lay a short distance offshore from the steep beach. I discovered, soon after stepping aboard our own sportfishing junk, that the contrivance, in the shallow inshore water, was a huge keepnet, containing hundreds of fish! The streamlined shapes were familiar and my companions confirmed that the fish were indeed tunny that are kept alive and fresh awaiting the market demand. Sashimi is a favourite popular dish – sliced, raw fish that the Japanese prefer to eat only fresh or iced-down to preserve the delicate flavour. It is strange to think that tunny caught abroad should be so highly valued that the Japanese are prepared to airfreight it home regardless of the transport costs!

We rounded the huge net and went on to a drift that would carry the junk parallel to the rocky coastline. I found, on dropping a lead, that we only had 30 feet or so under the keel. That didn't seem much for halibut, so obviously the local form must differ radically from the North Atlantic species. The baiting up, nevertheless, was not new to me for we used a minute live fish, something like an anchovy, hooked through the upper lip, reminiscent of the pollack fishing of Devon or Cornwall. The object, evidently, was to trundle the bait along the clean sandy bottom until it went solid. The flatfish could be expected to grab the livebait, hold it tight and then swallow it at leisure. Care had to be taken to give slack line immediately the grab was felt, otherwise the fish couldn't release its tight, killing hold without the angler tearing the bait away from it! This happened to me several times, causing our wizened skipper to shake his head vigorously in disapproval, until I got the hang of bait presentation and the strike.

The other anglers in the boat were taking a few fish, though not big specimens, and I realized that I needed to modify my ideas on halibut fishing, Atami style. The tackle – a spinning rod with fixed spool reel and 10-lb line – suggested that the fish wouldn't be large but I had been warned, quite

What a fantastic fishing boat! This traditional Atami junk, although
appearing top heavy, gave us an extremely stable platform . . .
I wondered how she would ride an Atlantic swell!

forcibly, that halibut fight like mad, and so it turned out. The 8-lb fish that I
eventually hooked really slogged it out in the shallow water! Although this
was average for these waters, one of the Japanese lads told me that the Pacific
halibut species *Hippoglossus stenolepsis* could be caught to much greater
weights in the north of the Japanese islands. Indeed, American, Russian and
indigenous fisheries have an enormous long-lining industry based on catches
of this single fish.

Because of the publicity given to Japanese global fishing activities, we think
of their commercial trawlers as enormous ocean-going catchers operating in
company with a massive factory ship. I was somewhat surprised, therefore, to
find that small junks were the mainstay of the home fisheries. There were
boats carrying nets and others with long-lining gear but much of the fishing
seemed to be with fixed traps. During several weeks in Japan, I saw no
evidence of commercial boats breaking inshore fishing regulations by trawling close in, as our boats are always doing. Sportfishing also seemed to enjoy a
far superior status to that accorded it in Britain – perhaps because its
contribution to providing food for the people is more highly valued.

Later in the morning's fishing, after the early mist at last left the water, we
found a greater quantity of fish on the feed. As further strikes came, I was
surprised that these halibut should choose to feed more deliberately as the
sun's strong light cut through the fairly shallow water. We discussed this
phenomenon and concluded that the halibut and other inshore species were
really attracted to the thrashing activities within the harbour's keepnets,
curious, perhaps, to investigate the rapid vibrations of the trapped fish. I had
quite a number of powerful takes, not all of them resulting in a hooked fish. I
think that I hooked one in three bites to end my boat session with five halibut!

While we fished from the junk, anglers were gathering along the shoreline,

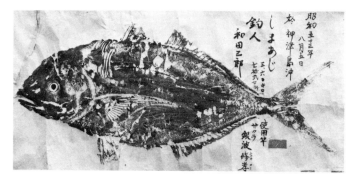

The Japanese way of remembering a good fish. A specimen is liberally smeared in a sort of quick-drying ink; then a piece of cotton cloth is smoothed over the contours of the fish to produce this perfect decoration for the wall of an angler's den.

particularly on rocky outcrops marking the sides of the bay and the harbour wall extensions. Interestingly, they weren't casting baits to be legered on the seabed. Each angler seemed to be armed with a very flexible rod about 16 feet long, with fixed spool reels and float rigs attached. The floats were fairly large and obviously heavy, which gave the weight to cast long distances.

The rods proved not to be as springy as I had assumed, but rather the weighty, 12–14-inch floats compressed their blanks on the cast to such a curve as to make them look floppy. The floats were sliders and the Atami anglers seemed to prefer the doubtful hooking qualities of their rig over our European system of casting a lead to the seabed, with a straight-through contact to the baited hook. After seeing them hook a lot of fish, I readjusted my ideas, concluding that either the delay in bite register on their float rigs was compensated for by the fact that they never struck early, pulling the hookbait away from a potential catch, or that the fish, provided given enough time, always took the bait positively.

Although the Japanese factories were churning out beachcasting rods for us to use in Britain, I didn't see one rod of this type in the hands of a local angler. I spent an hour watching and noticed an interesting casting style. Whereas we depend on 'Layback' or 'Pendulum' casting methods, the Japanese anglers used an 'Overhead' style accompanied by a 4–5-yard dash at the sea – rather like a javelin thrower in an athletics competition. Nor was there a wormbait in sight; tiny fish, dead or alive, were the only baits for the many species that I saw landed on that eventful day in the village of Atami.

CHAPTER THIRTEEN

The Tweed

SCOTLAND

Paddy Avery was a Yorkshireman. He lived in a small house on the bank of the Tweed at Norham, and he had the task of managing the fishings on this lower reach of the salmon river. Paddy and I fished together; in fact, he taught me most of what I know about salmon. Alas he is no longer alive. He was well aware of his heart problem and of the need to take things quietly, but he never let it interfere with his days on the river. Fishing was Paddy's life and I believe that he enjoyed every minute that he spent on the bank.

One particular day stands out from many others because on this occasion we both broke some of the rules that are sacrosanct in fishing for salmon.

A nice male fish for Avery from the streamy water. Paddy's badly-mangled fly, neatly caught in the kyped-jaw of the salmon, took a perfect hold and stayed fast.

The River Tweed, upstream from Norham Castle. There was a very fast current, running in a channel, beneath the undercut bank . . . and there were the lies.

Whenever I visited Paddy, he never greeted me in the conventional way but always started by giving me a brief resumé about the condition of the river. After a long drive from the south, it was evening when I arrived. Immediately he informed me of the low water condition, and that there were fish in the pools that didn't seem to be moving on up toward the higher stretches beyond Coldstream. So, in the late autumn sunlight that pierced the gloom of his parlour, we got straight into the business of arranging our angling effort for the following day. Paddy, as always, had got on the telephone immediately things looked right for a settled spell. This time a lot of fish were being held in the lower pools in extremely low water, and the warm autumn weather pattern seemed promising for a few days fishing.

Next morning we were at the pool above the stone bridge that crosses between England and Scotland. There was a groyne (Paddy called it a 'cauld') upstream by the island which split the force of the water. It had become a favourite first cast for me over the years. In times of low water, a patch of streamer weed grew on the Scottish side. Underwater variation on the riverbed threw a boil to the surface at this point, almost as if there was a boulder or some other obstruction that caused a visible but smaller area of troubled water.

The aim was to cast square to let the fly fish round from the far bank, through the roughened water, close into the edge of the weedbed. Once there, the fly had to be lifted before it swam into the weeds that just showed at the surface. But before I could get to my spot, Paddy insisted that I fish down from the tail of the upper pool, where dace flitted in the shallows below the groyne. He always maintained, and I had once seen it for myself, that salmon chased the dace in the shallows continuously, offering the chance of a taking fish at that point in the river. Late on the previous evening he had spotted a fish rising in the shallows, apparently circling the pool, always returning to the same lie. I tried, but nothing came to me, possibly because I was eager to get down to my hotspot and wasn't seriously giving attention to the casting or the way in which the fly behaved.

While I waded the river, Paddy sat quietly on the high grassy bank. Sometimes murmuring advice but often scoffing at my casting attempts, his eyes rarely left the water as he searched all his known lies for signs of a fish. A cast, fish it round and then a pace downstream is the procedure for flyfishing on any salmon river. I followed the rules and gradually got back into the discipline of laying the line out cleanly, followed by a generous upstream mend to allow the bait to swim round with good presentation. I had chosen a small, tattered, almost unrecognizable Dunkeld tied on to a double-hook, for no other reason than the fly had been good to me on previous visits!

About twenty minutes into my fishing I heard Paddy shout that he was leaving to follow some of his other rods downstream to a spot where they would spend the day. Seeing him begin the long walk that was likely to take him an hour or more, I began to relax into my own way of casting and working the fly. After so long away from casting with a double-handed, lengthy rod, I must admit that the whole business was pretty erratic. I am positive that the only way to become a proficient caster and salmon fisher is to live right alongside the river. This enables you to cast with fluency, know the behaviour of the species intimately and, most importantly, be around at peak times for the running of the fresh fish. Travelling to any salmon river for just a few days fishing in a year can only be described as gambling on very long odds!

I had been casting reasonably well for about half an hour when I saw my first fish turn at the fly. It rose at a point behind the lure and turned flashing silver in the light, bringing its tail over in a curve that sent a splash across the streamy water. Excitedly I fished out the cast, stripped some line back and lifted from the water. Retreating a pace upstream, I sent the fly out to cover the water once more, intending to bring it round a little shorter on its travel to see if the fish, with a longer, clearer view, would rise again.

After mending the line, the fly came round perfectly on its course. I saw nothing but felt the positive draw as the fish came to the fly, took it and turned. Controlling my anxiety, I remembered to give it line – a few seconds as the salmon sank down through the water. Feeling pressure of the pull increasing, I reacted to it by lifting the rod tip and holding reasonably strongly. The fish was on and running.

There was little in the way of spectacular fighting from this fish; it simply

moved across the streamy water and began short runs upstream. This is an
ideal direction for a fish to move as it has to fight both rod and pressure from
the water flow. Paddy's advice to me about playing salmon was always to
hold them fairly hard and play them out in the shortest possible time, on the
theory that a salmon allowed to 'do its own thing' was often in command of
the fight. I have met anglers who were in such fright of losing a salmon that
they fought their fish too gently, giving them an opportunity to shed the
hook.

I kept a steady pressure on my fish, encountering few difficulties, and it
came to the gaff within ten minutes. Out of the river, I carried the fish, which
weighed around 12 lbs, up the steep bank and laid it on the grass for despatch.
Once done, I covered the fish with my jacket, an innocent action that was to
cause quite a few hilarious moments when Paddy returned, just after I had
waded back into the water, to give me the benefit of some more advice.

I saw him coming out of the corner of my eye. He took a seat on the highest
part of the bank and sat quietly watching, doubtless thinking that my
thrashing the water into a lather had some sort of planning behind it. I fished
on for a spell but nothing moved in the river. Paddy intimated that it might be
time to try a cast or two below the bridge as obviously I'd still a lot to learn
about salmon fishing. He shouted that I ought to have a cast where the river
was far wider, at a place where a huge tree trunk, probably loosened by a
storm the previous winter from the bankside somewhere upriver, lay in the
stream. As the Tweed widened, it became shallower, so that the tree could no
longer trundle downstream to the sea.

Gazing down the river from the parapet of the stone bridge, Paddy had
noticed the odd resident fish near the tree, usually rising at the edge of the
streamy water created by the interruption of the river's flow. However, the lie
seemed impossible to fish from either bank. On one side the tree was close in,
with fish rising beyond it, whereas a cast from the far bank would bring the fly
round far too quickly, at a speed that could only show it for a second or so to a
waiting fish. Paddy suggested taking the boat down to fish from slightly
above the tree, although that made it difficult to position the boat. Nevertheless we thought we would give it a try.

Gathering my gear together, I asked Paddy if he wouldn't mind carrying
my jacket. He grabbed it up and was about to be off when the glint of scales
caught his eye. 'You lousy tyke,' he roared. 'Here's me thinking that I'd have
to get on to the water myself to make sure that you had one fish at least to take
home!' 'Paddy me lad,' I said, 'It isn't a kelt, it didn't die of natural causes and
came from just the spot that you always guide me to.' That seemed to placate
him but the muttering continued for the ten minutes that it took us to reach
the bridge.

Down to the bank we went and loaded the minimum of clutter aboard. Our
first few harsh words came over who would handle the oars. Knowing of

Paddy Avery leans into his salmon, fished on a single-handed seatrout
rod, as it fights in the streamy water where the river narrows and the
current speeds.

Paddy's health problem, I indicated that it was only reasonable for me to take us downstream, thinking that Paddy could then take over to put me over the lie and I'd row back later against the current. Well, that wasn't how it was to be: Paddy Avery insisted that this was his river, I was just a guest (probably another of his names for somebody with a lot to learn) and that he was in charge. Eager to get at the fishing, I gave way to my irascible friend.

We drifted downstream, with an occasional pull on the oars to fetch the boat up to the massive branches that emerged above water. Paddy's thought was to keep the boat aligned upstream of the tree and for me to cast across the river with a fairly long line that would bring the fly tight against the faster current. Three times I tried doing that, and three times the fly fouled and was somehow lost. Then I had a brainwave, or at least the glimmer of an idea. 'Paddy, hand me over my bag,' I asked. 'I'll change to my sinking line, then we can go in closer, see where the branches are but get down clear of them with the fly.' The idea that I should attempt to change lines on a 14-foot fly rod in a 12-foot dinghy just about caused him to riot!

'It's easy Paddy, I'll only have to break the rod down into sections, run the line through each bit and then build it up, with you holding the butt for me.' I didn't catch his reply, doubtless a little snippet from Yorkshire.

Anyway, after a lot of cussing and far too much noise, as the rod and our other traps banged around on the duckboards, we managed to get the rod rerigged. The first cast showed the vast difference in behaviour of the two lines. The floater had swum the fly high in the stream but my sinker appeared too heavy, with the lure scraping the bed of the river. 'That's about as useful as a frig at the North Pole!' was my companion's immediate comment. However, I persevered, especially as at that moment a fish rose just beyond the end of the tree downstream. I was in a quandary. The sinking line allowed us to fish a shorter line and control the fly close into the branches that stuck up through the surface, but it sank too low in the water.

I asked Paddy to drop the boat back a little, just enough for me to reach the spot where I'd seen the fish rise. With only a cast of a few yards I could let the line go down and then lift the rod so that it fished the fly 'sink and draw'. I got away with the first cast but the second elicited the cutting remark that I was 'feathering for salmon', though what else could he expect from an ignorant blighter known for his confessed love of sea angling?

I wouldn't be drawn into an argument about the ethics of what I was doing or how the 'rules' were being bent, because as far as I could see I was casting a genuine fly and working it, the tactics being far removed from spinning! Before we had a chance to develop the discussion further, a salmon took charge by giving the fly a tremendous belt, hooking itself solidly and dashing off across the river like a mad thing. Immediately Paddy's face lit up and he shouted his encouragement as though the whole episode was running to his own plan.

Tweed fish don't seem to run very large in the autumn and mine was no exception, but it gave us both a fight to remember. The fish used the whole river and we could only follow as best the current and the unwieldy boat would allow. I didn't see more than a flash of silver for ten minutes or so. It was as if the salmon knew that it had done a stupid thing. The lie was perfect and couldn't be got at unless the 'rules' were swept aside, and yet this fish just had to have a go!

After a few more minutes, dear old Paddy got me ashore to where I was able to get some control, and together we beached the fish. Only then did he tell me to take a glance at the very high, treed bank where he had seen the inevitable watcher – the character that always seems to be hanging around on the river, hiding in the undergrowth and who carries the message to the local pub that so-and-so has a fish.

We packed up for the afternoon to give ourselves a rest before changing beats for the later evening spell. Once again we broke with tradition by fishing single-handed trout rods for the hell of it. Paddy had a beautiful cock fish and I managed to disgrace myself by losing all three fish that came to my fly. How I miss Paddy Avery and his use of those few, concise phrases and knowing nods that told you how much he wanted you to get into a fish!

CHAPTER FOURTEEN

The Corrie Creature

SCOTLAND

I have always been a stickler for trying to make a correct identification of fish that I have caught or seen. This means giving the catch more than just a cursory glance. I once asked a well-known sea angler, who was happily engaged in feathering for mackerel, what colour the species was. I stopped him turning round for a quick peep into the fishbox, and he found the simple task of colour description almost impossible. When I pointed out that he must have caught thousands of that particular fish over the years, he readily agreed that he and probably many other anglers rarely take more than a quick look at their fish.

Sometimes, however, we come across a situation and a rarity that defies adequate explanation; and often the occurrence so varies from the norm that we dismiss it or keep quiet for fear that our sanity will be questioned.

I had an experience, years back, that I have only talked of recently, encouraged by reading of similar experiences by highly regarded writers. I leave it to you, the reader, to make your own decision as to its validity.

I was fishing for haddock, with Mike Shepley, off the Isle of Arran. Our dinghy was drifting on an oily-smooth sea, over 9 fathoms of water, off the Corrie shore, just outside the Bay of Brodick. The evening was beautiful, little cloud cover and a half-light that allowed us to see for miles. Mike and I had caught a few small haddies while we chatted away and enjoyed a simple fishing that was lazy yet productive.

We were suddenly alerted to a noisy splashing ahead of the boat's bow. A glance showed that there was considerable disturbance to the surface about 50 yards farther out in deeper water. Our immediate thought was of a shoal of

My impression of the Corrie creature. Although memories blur, I can still feel the shiver that ran through me as I watched it swim.

A common seal and her pup
Phoca vitulina.

mackerel, a breaching basking shark or a bunch of seals, all of them distinct possibilities in the Firth of Clyde, and all subsequently discounted, in the light of our experience, as unlikely.

The ruffled water settled back to smoothness and we were both able to see, clearly, what appeared to be a head and a long body break the water's skin. The head was rounded, and then came a gap of a couple of feet, suggesting a neck, before the larger, thicker bulk of the body. The creature seemed to me to move in a series of undulating motions: not the side to side (horizontal plane) swimming movements of a fish but more the up and down (vertical plane) progress of a mammal, such as a porpoise. I recall that the head was only slightly raised above the apparent level of the body mass. I cannot say that I saw any evidence of fins, either dorsally or otherwise. Overall size is difficult to judge when something is moving away from you, yet I would suggest that it was longer than our boat, making it over 17 feet long.

The observation wasn't a fleeting glimpse; we watched for several minutes. All this time the thing was on the surface and swimming in a straight line toward the Scottish mainland. I have since had many thoughts about this sighting, none of them given any added dimension until reading Gavin Maxwell's account of similar happenings in his book about the sharkfishing industry, *Harpoon at a Venture*, wherein he recounts the experiences of a number of Hebridean folk and quotes other sightings of creatures not, as yet, explained by science.*

Neither Mike Shepley nor I have diluted our opinions as to what we saw. After many years the sighting remains as clear as on that alcohol-free evening in Arran. I have since seen a great many other marine mammals, such as whales and porpoises, but never has there been any similarity in their behaviour to that of the 'Corrie creature'!

---

* I have, over years of research, read of many creature sightings around the world. Those observations for the British Isles, and the Scottish west coast in particular, further convince me that what I saw was a creature that has been around for a long time. Its appearance in the Firth of Clyde, perhaps off the Isle of Arran, is nothing new!

*   *   *   *   *

I would recommend *Sea Serpents, Sailors and Sceptics* by Graham J. McEwan: Routledge & Kegan Paul as further reading on this fascinating subject. Mr McEwan offers us 41 sightings in British waters in the last century, along with a fascinating sequence of sightings and descriptions of world-wide events! Oddly enough, quite a number are in the vicinity of Scotland's islands.

The following extract from this book gives intriguing information about the long-necked seal, of which he mentions 94 probable sightings.

Distinguishing features
Long neck
Small seal-like head
Bulky body, lacking distinct tail
Four large flippers
Vertical undulations

This creature seems to be covered in thick rolls of fat, the appearance varying somewhat to the displacement of this fat, showing one, two or three big humps. The head is small, resembling that of a dog or seal, and apparently lengthening as the animal grows older. The eyes are small and there are often two small horns mentioned by observers. These horns are possibly horny protuberances and may be an aid to breathing or to prevent bubbles from obscuring the animal's vision as it exhales underwater. The neck is long and flexible. There are two pairs of flippers, sometimes seen through clear water from above, and occasionally when the animal has been seen ashore. There seems to be no distinct tail, but the hind flippers may resemble a bilobate tail, or, when held together as sometimes seals do, a fish tail. The skin looks smooth when wet and seen from a distance, but closer observation reveals it to be wrinkled and rough, sometimes showing what looks like coarse fur. It is dark on top, sometimes mottled, and lighter underneath. It seems to be between 30 and 70 feet long.

The animal can swim very quickly, attaining speeds of 35 knots, suggesting that it is a predator which chases fish.

It is found all over the world except polar seas, and the correlation between sightings and climate indicates that it likes warm but not hot regions.

This creature seems very likely to be a pinniped. The webbed feet or flippers, the absence of a tail, and in a few sightings its movement on land – bounding like a sea-lion – point to this conclusion. In addition there is a greasy wake, also a characteristic of pinnipeds (seals).

CHAPTER FIFTEEN

Icebergs, Arctic Char and Nostalgia

GREENLAND

Flying across massive, powder-blue glaciers and windswept snowfields, pierced by granite peaks, I had my first sight of the remote airfield at Narssarssuaq. The Americans who constructed it at the beginning of the Second World War simply called it 'Bluey West One', doubtless having trouble in wrapping their tongues around the Eskimo words. Using a bit of imagination, one could almost hear the roar of Flying Fortresses and Liberators as they ran up their engines for the last leg of the flight to war-torn Britain. Now, in 1976, evidence of their presence lay in the jumbled 'graveyard' of engines, trucks and airplane carcasses lying beyond the airstrip. Across the fjord lies Qagssiarssuk where Erik the Red established his

Flying into Greenland, the plane crosses vast glaciers, passing huge mountain peaks that protrude through the inland icefield, before arriving at the warm, coastal fjord.

Ingeborg's Pool where spawning char struggle to reach the gravel beds
that form their breeding habitat – rarely finding enough flowing water
to ease their journey.

Norse settlement in the year 985. A ruined cowshed and the foundations of a
church, established by Erik's wife Tjodhild at Brattalid, have been absorbed
into the sheep-rearing farms of this fertile, coastal belt.

On this corner of Greenland, the strip of soil that follows each mountain
contour around the craggy coastline is truly green. Many enormous glaciers,
slowly melting, send a rush of ice water into hundreds of tiny streams, with
stony beds, that are the haunt of arctic char. This member of the salmon family
spends most of its life in the surrounding ocean, feeding on krill and other
planktonic creatures. Spawning usually takes place in August, and the fish,
when ready to breed, swim up into the fjords to seek feeder streams that are
free of ice, some of them containing hardly enough water to cover the fish's
backs!

I had come to Greenland to make a film on the country and its fishing.
Along with Michael Shepley and his fellow Scot, Paul Young, we intended to
walk into the mountains to pools reputed to hold many char waiting to find
enough depth of water to let them spawn. Our first task was to arrange
backpacks that would hold filming equipment, a small quantity of fishing
tackle and a bite of food. We were helped, in selecting and carrying the gear,
by our Greenlandic guide Frederik, a mountain of a man with shoulders

nearly as wide as a door and stout legs that told of countless miles spent trudging across a landscape that has no roads or public transport.

Ingeborg's Pool, which was to be our first taste of char fishing, was only about an acre in size, filled by ice-melt and emptied by a rocky stream that was only a few inches in depth. How the fish manage to swim upstream from the saltwater fjord is hard to say, but clearly, given that the Greenland summer is only a few months long, a sense of urgency compels them to make the most hazardous ascents.

Paul, an international fly fisherman with a deserved reputation, forced a strong pace as we stumbled up the rocky incline that led from the shore of Erik's Fjord. Throughout our flight from Copenhagen, Mike had regaled us with what we assumed were exaggerated stories of the char and their fighting qualities, and doubtless they really got through to Paul who was determined to be the first to make a cast across water that had never before seen a fly rod!

Offloading the precious camera gear, we fumbled with trembling fingers to tie on our flies, each of us glancing at the others to check on the pattern considered suitable for our first efforts. As it happened, anything would have served us equally well. Within seconds of his first cast, Paul had a take that arched the rod, fiercely pulling line from the drum, and he promptly applied the wearing-down tactics demanded by a strong, Scottish brown trout. The

Our first arctic char from the pool; hard, fleshy and colourful, these fish will attack any bait presented to them, taking with a fierce jerk to the rod tip.

char reacted by leaping clear of the water, making vigorous runs toward a waterfall that spilled over a rockface shaded from the sun. That fish fought for what seemed an hour before it came to the extended net, having completely exhausted itself in the process.

We were quickly to learn that char often fight to the death and that a protracted battle between angler and fish is unwise if the latter is to be released. With few exceptions, notably some plump fish that we needed to cook over a glowing brushwood fire, all of our Greenland char were shaken off the hook and returned to freedom.

Mike had tied on a well-dressed wet fly (as I remember it was a March Brown) that was taken with alacrity by a brightly coloured cock fish in glowing-red breeding pelage. My choice of fly was a Jersey Herd, as I thought the char might be feeding on their own fry, there being no evidence of insect life on the water or even in the tangled scrub that grew in sparse patches along the watercourse.

My fly was wrenched away at speed by a fish that showed for a moment through the surface film. It was a female, clothed in silvery scales dotted with white spots; and she proved that arctic char, no matter their size, can equal any freshwater fish for speed or determination to shed the hook. We could have taken fish after fish at Ingeborg's Pool but we decided to trudge around the stony shore of the upper fjord to where the Quingua River spilled its milky-white water into the sea. The milkiness is apparently caused by the melting of old ice and the gradual process of the moving glacier grinding rocks into mud as it moves seaward.

We lost our flies, in the sense that they disappeared from sight when only an inch or so below the water's surface. I had my doubts about char seeing, let alone taking, a fly in this rushing stream. This seemed to be borne out by a party of West German anglers who arrived festooned in spinning rods and flashy waistcoats that held an array of lures. Apparently they knew the Quingua River and that its char were disposed to grabbing large spinners if rapidly wound in across the river. A few minutes spent watching the lads fish undoubtedly proved the value of their tactics; but a high proportion of the fish that I saw hooked and landed had the bait snagged into the outside of the jaw or in the flanks. Probably the char saw the fluttering bait for only a split second, went hard at it and then tried to turn away but were hooked by the speed of retrieve and the press of tumbling water.

We persevered with our flyfishing to no avail. During the long tramp back to our boat, which is the only transport system capable of negotiating the fjords that indent Greenland's coastal belt, we made plans with Frederik to fish on the following day on a small stream. He knew one with a steady flow and deep pools little affected by the milky water from the inland ice field.

Although Greenland was hot during the hours of daylight, the evenings were cool. We felt grateful for another American structure, the Arctic Hotel,

The airport river (the stream deserves a better name) at Narssarssuaq has just a few connected pools but the clear water gave us perfect vision of the shoals.

which is a conversion of the wartime officers' mess into a comfortable hostelry. The evening meal, a galaxy of Danish and traditional Greenland food, was enlivened by the noise made by a party of boisterous hill-walkers whose tents had blown down in the wild winds that tend to roar in every evening from the iceberg-strewn fjord. Soon the fishy conversation was sprinkled with Dutch, German, Icelandic and various Scandinavian tongues. The hardy trampers found it difficult to understand why we anglers had to travel to the arctic wastes to catch fish. We, in turn, couldn't see why anybody would choose to torture their bodies walking Greenland's rigorous terrain – and not have a rod in their hands!

Early in the morning we prepared to copy our new-found friends in a cross-country hike to Frederik's stream. What he failed to tell us beforehand was that most of the journey would consist of stepping from the top of one rock to another. The path to our fishing lay across a moraine, a continuous field of smooth pebbles left by the passage of a glacier. We stumbled and fell repeatedly but eventually reached our pools, strung in magical beauty along a stream that wound its way across the glacier bed between sheer walls of a rocky defile. Tackled up, we cast our flies into much calmer water than the previous day's fishing had provided, the surface so still that one could

Paul Young and the author with their catch of char from the river. Most were taken on fly, with just one or two fished, as an experiment, on a blade spinner.

actually see a char rise to inspect the fly. The fish swam in shoals, backwards and forwards between the shallows that separated the individual pools. Paul, Mike and I hooked into fish within minutes. The fly pattern didn't seem to matter as long as there was a flash of red, and a hint of silver body. Char after char hit the flies, tore through the pool, sending the main shoal scattering, were played and beached. This activity did not appear to frighten the rest of the fish after their initial reaction. They settled back into a routine of patrolling, across the water, from margin to margin.

After taking a succession of fish on the fly, I turned my attention to the light spinning rod, thinking that a spinning lure might urge one of the larger specimens to attack. I'd seen quite a few really big char that alternately rose to the surface and then sank into the deeper, darker water. Putting up a small blade spinner, I walked into the shallows at the head of the deepening pool. The first cast drew a fish that followed the lure almost to my boots. Repeated casts brought exactly the same reaction from fish large and small. As the take, when stripping a fly, had been a fast no-nonsense affair, I decided to speed up the retrieve of the lure. At one point of my reeling in, the rod tip thumped over and stayed in a working curve. A char rose from the water about 30 yards out into the pool and crashed on to its flank in a flurry of spray. One short glimpse had established that it was a fair-sized cock fish in splendid spawning colours.

That fish gave me the works. Apparently oblivious to the fighting strain exerted by the rod, the fish cut across the pool, nylon slicing the surface like a breadknife. Our battle went on for more than five minutes: each time I thought I had the fish under control, it produced another burst of energy that took it far off into the deeper water. Feeling a little guilty at putting the fish to so much stress before beaching it, I decided that this char had to grace the frying-pan. It was a perfect size for the campfire meal that we had all promised ourselves.

Frederik, munching his way through fried char and wholemeal bread, explained that there were other places and different methods to fish for char. He surprised us all by suggesting that we spend our final day in Greenland fishing for a strange mixture of cod and char in deepish water close into the shoreline of Erik's Fjord where there were a few small icebergs. Spinning was to be the taking method, and he guaranteed that a fast retrieve, on the surface, would hook char, while a slower, deeper return would take the lure down to the cod that lurked closer to the bottom. When I enquired why it was considered worth fishing next to an iceberg, Frederik assured us that the char like to use the cover afforded by the berg, and that there were always tiny creatures, probably shrimps, that the char fed on amid the floating ice.

Our last day found us at Helicopter Bay, where a shingle strand inclined down into deepwater. Only a few small icebergs could be seen, most of them tiny and blown up on to the shingle where they had stranded on the receding tide. Short casts were enough to get among loose clumps of floating ice that

drifted by on the slow current that is ever-present at the upper limits of the fjord. Mike had a plump char in two casts; it didn't attempt to go deep but played just under the surface in short, lateral runs.

Someone, inevitably, had to weaken, to leave the char and sink a lure down to where cod ought to lie. Paul got the first fish. Small but lively, it had the general appearance of the cod from more southerly sea areas yet with different marbling on the flanks. It was, in fact, a separate species *Gadus ogac*, new to all three of us, that appeared far fatter in body shape. We were interested to note the contemptuous reaction to this small cod by the local inhabitants, who do not consider it worth eating!

Both char and the small codfish are harassed by Greenland sharks, a

Erik's Fjord always has a gathering of
icebergs at the mouths of rivers entering it.
The larger bergs break away from glaciers to
ground in shallow water.

An arctic cod species *Gadus ogac* plump yet
not quite as tasty as the Atlantic fish. The
colouring is a dark brown with light fawn
marbling.

coldwater species that enters the fjords whenever spawning char gather. The flesh of this shark is poisonous when fresh, so the local Eskimo fishermen dry it before any is eaten. The shark is mainly valued for its liver oil and incredibly strong skin, both products being exported to Europe.

One fishing expedition we would like to have made was to the Qorqup River with its run of salmon. This river is fed by a lake, which in turn gets a constant supply of freshwater from the melting glacier above it. Unfortunately there were too many packed icebergs on the day that we boated up to take a look, but we were sufficiently impressed to promise ourselves a future visit and to have another opportunity to taste the wild wind and walk the stark wilderness of the world's largest island.

Narssarssuaq 1985 . . . the return

People often say that it is a mistake to walk down Memory Lane. Well, that's as may be but some months ago I grabbed the opportunity when my dear friend, Eiler Hansen of the Danish Tourist Board, called me up to say that there was a chance of returning to Greenland. To travel in exactly the same way and to the same area that I had visited eight years before – I couldn't pack the gear fast enough!

Only the aircraft type had changed on the flight from Copenhagen. Now it was the much bigger DC8, carrying a mixed complement of hikers, fishers and pinstripe-suited businessmen out across the North Sea. We passed over the Faroes, flew south of Iceland which lay clear to see on the starboard horizon and continued westward to find the icy sea-fjords of Greenland.

This is one flight where passengers take little notice of the cabin staff requesting them to keep to their seats. Each window had three heads jammed together peering through the tiny orifice. Cameras clicked away frantically and there were gasps of surprise as each glacier slid below the cruising plane. Tremendous mountain peaks pierced the inland icefield, in many places said to be hundreds of metres deep, like Swiss Alps appearing through a cloud layer!

Our approach to the wartime airfield hadn't changed a bit. In fact, a further element of excitement was added as our pilot warned us not to be too alarmed by sudden changes in airspeed as he applied the airbrakes to aid a swift descent into the tight flightpath up Erik's Fjord. We were surprised, however, to find, on landing, that Narssarssuaq now boasted a terminal building. There was a notice reading 'Customs and Passport Control' but no sign of anyone sufficiently interested to do those jobs. A van carried the luggage away and I thought that I would walk the kilometre or so to the Arctic Hotel. Another change here, although one for the better; they had built a new wing with a superb dining room and lounge.

I never seem to be at a fishing place anywhere for more than five minutes before somebody, seeing the fishing tackle, remarks that I should have arrived 'last Wednesday week'. This time it was 'We've had no snow!' I couldn't quite work that one out until it was explained that at least two of the rivers and Ingeborg's Pool get their waterflow from melting snow rather than a constant stream of ice water from one or other of the many glaciers. Too little snow meant that a lot of the feeder streams, with clear water suitable for flyfishing, had almost dried up. The char were hanging around at the mouth of the rivers either in the saltwater or in the white, turbid stream that only suited spinning. Added to this problem, there was a thinly veiled suggestion that our hosts, the Greenland villagers, had got themselves a mess of nylon gillnets and had strung them across the mouths of the rivers that emptied into the sea-fjords!

Slightly discouraged, our party, which was made up of Dutch magazine and newspapermen, arranged to fish Ingeborg's Pool on the following day; but first we all wanted to make the enthralling boat trip up the Qoroq Fjord to see the glacier and get among real icebergs. I had made the trip twice before, on my earlier visit to Greenland, yet the voyage was somehow different. I can only think that the bergs and the colours are never the same on succeeding days. Arctic light, so clear and blue, throws every facet of an iceface into fantastic relief, colours altering with every small change in the sun's position.

Our first morning was bright and slightly chilly, just right for a brisk walk across the tundra from the landing place to Ingeborg's Pool. There is always a walk to any of the fishings because the available transport, in our case a beautiful sea-going launch, can only land anglers where there is deep water for the boat to glide in and nudge her bow against the high rocks. Then it's a careful jump ashore, a cheery wave and off to the hills – with everything carried on one's back!

Returning to a faraway fishing water gives me a creepy feeling. Too much optimistic musing at home in the armchair and a modicum of boasting to the other members of the party *en passage* demand that all goes well. You've guessed it! The pool wasn't the same in area, well down from its former remembered level, and my spirits nosedived correspondingly. Even so, we caught char – not as many as on my earlier trip, just enough to give the lads a feel for the quality of the fight and, incidently, a quick bite as we grilled a few fish over a smoky fire.

With six rods covering the pool, it wasn't long before the fishing died. We only had two days to get among fish, so we opted for the sea-fjord, which meant taking the spinning rods to some huge rocks that jutted out into the deepwater. There should have been a fair run of char, in view of the fact that the shoals could not get into many low-water streams, but in any event the char refused to show, their place being taken by Greenland cod.

I would never recommend to game fishers that they spin for cod with 5-lb line, but that is what the lads had to do. They started by hitting into fish of

Guido Vinck, former world casting champion from Belgium, stretches for his first Greenland char taken on the fly in the deeper water of Ingeborg's Pool.

The seabed of the fjord was covered with a veritable carpet of sea scorpions . . . and the species apparently took a liking to Mepps spinners whirling over their heads!

about 5–6 lbs. Then the cod disappeared to be replaced by some of the finest sea scorpions that I have ever seen. The first fish, taken by the travel editor of 'De Telegraaf', Harry Muller, gave an unexpectedly superb fight, weighing in at 5 lbs. If that fish was representative of the fjord's population of sea scorpions, there are clearly sea angling records for the smashing!

Our cod soon returned in numbers, most of them hitting the spoon baits like bass. It seemed that these fish would rise clear of the bed of the fjord to take the fluttering bait. Even the novice anglers who started winding as soon as the bait hit the surface caught cod, in at least 30 feet of water. Remembering what the locals had said about the eating quality of Greenland cod, I lit a fire,

A tasty bonus for any fishing day – to eat part of the catch of
shrimp-fed char. The sizzling fillets never tasted dry but were always
smooth and oily.

wrapped a couple of fish in some kitchen foil and tossed them into the
glowing embers. They weren't the best thing that I'd ever tasted, being
slightly watery and lacking firmness, yet my companions tucked in with
enthusiasm, probably proving the fishermen's adage that everything tastes
better eaten in the open air.

We returned to our hotel weary but eager for the tramp across the glacier
bed to the clear waters of the Airport River, scheduled for the following
morning.

Our first task was to cross the river at its lower reaches. The bed of the
stream was composed of smooth, round pebbles about 8 inches in diameter. I
found everything on the move as I felt gingerly with the toe of my wader. The
stones were constantly rolling downstream in the murky, rushing torrent,
and indeed the milkiness of the stream was our difficulty, preventing a clear
view of the riverbed.

Our river-crossing antics would have made a superb Chaplin movie and I
longed for the loan of a wading staff! Having overcome the stream, we spent
the next half hour lowering our pulse rates while crossing the pebbled
moraine. Here and there tiny alpine flowers grew in patches, where a large
boulder afforded some measure of protection from the biting winds that can
come roaring down from the inland ice. We found the clear water pools much
as I expected them to be – devoid of a constant flow and considerably lower
than on my earlier visit.

The first cast was a textbook one! Hardly had the spoon hit the water than a flashy, spawn-red char rocketed upwards. Looking to be about 2 lbs or more, the fish made scything runs through the surface film. I had visions of a massive catch, but it wasn't to be that easy, although we had quite a lot of sport, small fish that fought well, on both fly and spinners. Most of them came from darker areas of water, secluded spots where the pool was overshadowed by huge boulders and slabs of granite. The lack of snow, and its summer melting, was without doubt a vital factor in dispersing the fish through the pools.

Those of us who wandered off to make a few casts in the adjacent main river had better-sized fish, though not in any numbers. Two days was not sufficient time even for a so-called press visit, particularly when fish had to be searched for; obviously they have to spawn, and in low-water times even the local Greenland fishermen have difficulty in locating the new holding areas.

We did find, during our short time in Greenland, that the char are constant, ever present in the waters that suit their spawning requirements, as in streams with a big concentration of loose floating ice at the mouth. There they are safe from netting and can choose when to enter the feeders. Flyfishing is still more productive than spoons, and I believe that it leaves the pools less disturbed. Again, my choice of fly would be for something with a hint of red, silver-bodied or gold-bodied, with a black hackle to give outline when the water is at all milky.

Our luck was really in on the tramp back to cross the river. A member of the Danish Meteorological Station's staff had been fishing with his wife and small son higher up the stream. He offered a dry and safe trip across in his boat, even though he had to row the tumbling water three or four times. You see, fishing is a sport of gentlemen!

CHAPTER SIXTEEN

A Touch of Angling Witchcraft

IRELAND

Only the tiniest stub of the float showed above the surface of the canal; with a tremble it moved sideways and lifted a fraction of an inch. I struck to feel the weight of the fish kicking as I raised the rod tip to draw the bream out from among the shoal. It was my first hooked fish after a maddening succession of line bites. My companion, hunched down on his chair in the bankside reed thicket, called softly, 'They've got their heads down now.'

There are times when an angler is forced to travel alone to a faraway place,

The Grand Canal at Ticknevin, Co. Kildare. Downstream of the lock there are beautiful swims, of even depth, always producing bream and rudd shoals.

finding himself on a strange bank without helpful criteria. All he can do is to fall back on an accumulated fund of knowledge from past fishing days.

After an invitation to travel to Kildare, my canal fishing education began with a vengeance. I had absolutely no previous experience of this type of fishing, yet I had something better, more valuable – a man who had volunteered to give me his time and, as it turned out, the urge to refresh myself by returning there every year.

The Grand Canal, at Prosperous in the east of Ireland, had been steadily gaining a reputation as a water that holds a superb head of coarse fish. It starts life in the heart of the city of Dublin, and meanders across Ireland's midland plain to spill into the River Shannon.

I'd never fished a stretch of water like it before. Living in East Anglia, where there are few waters that resemble a canal, I viewed them as stillwaters, of even depth, with fish just about anywhere! Although most canals are provided with a system of locks, which do serve to separate the water into chunks, fish can roam over huge distances, so that one of the hardest tasks for any fisherman is to locate fish in what can appear to be a featureless environment.

Without doubt, I was incredibly lucky to meet Gordon Dickinson. A native of Northumbria, he'd chosen to make Ireland his home. Gordon is both a

technician by trade and in his approach to his sport. He set about fishing the canal in a schematic fashion, discovering the major shoals of bream, establishing areas holding tench and locating the rudd. Then it was a matter of applying constantly varying tactics learned on his home fisheries until he came up with a successful formula for fishing on the Irish canals.

My first session with Gordon began on the evening of my arrival at the village of Prosperous. There was to be no first visit to the pub, standard practice in Ireland. Out to the canal we went, but not to fish. He took me through narrow lanes, on to towpaths and across bogland, merely to inspect the water! Each stretch of canal was analysed, with an account of how it fished, when and what could be expected. This intimate knowledge astonished me; the man seemed to know every bed of reeds, applying individual names – 'The Red Gates', 'The Tree Struck by Lightning', to favoured swims.

Early next morning, after breakfast at Sheila O'Brien's guesthouse, we ventured out to the village of Ticknevin. To me, the canal looked exactly the same along its entire length. There were slight variations in width, and reeds grew more strongly in one or two places, but I could see no pitch that deserved attention more than any other. Dickinson halted the car about 100 yards short of the lock, opposite old iron farm gates. This was to be his swim; mine, he suggested, lay 10 yards or so further along the open bank.

Gordon began putting up his rod while taking a keen look at how I was setting up. He didn't like my idea of a float; I'd gone for an antenna but he pointed out that the pull on this canal tended to vary according to the amount of water that the lock keepers allowed through the sluices. 'Your antenna will be hard to control,' he remarked. 'Try this,' and he handed me a 6-inch chunk of peacock quill from among the mass of floats bundled up in his box. 'It will handle the variation in flow when it starts. Shot it down to give about an eighth of an inch showing.'

I'd never in my life fished a float shotted so carefully! Then came advice about what to expect as bites. 'I always shot for lift bites,' Dickinson went on. 'Practically all the bream bites are lifts, with the occasional sharp pull. When that happens, it's odds on the fish is a skimmer.'

I settled in to the swim, casting to where the reeds, growing out from the opposite bank, bulged into the water. Initial plumbing for depth indicated that a slight shelf existed about 3 feet out from the reed margin. It seemed a good place to make a start. Suddenly my ears were assaulted by a fearful racket, as an old tractor came trundling down the bank. The noise, accompanied by vibration which made the whole pitch tremble, had no effect on Gordon's concentration. The tractor stopped behind us and a cheery voice asked how we were doing – something that would produce a scowl in Britain, but not here. It seemed impossible to me that fish, however used to vibration, could tolerate the fearful din!

Later, after some years of familiarity with the canal, noise ceased to bother

Gordon Dickinson with fish from the Grand Canal. Bream, rudd and
perch predominate, yet every new season finds more hybrids and roach
in the angler's catch!

me. Youngsters would tear down the bank on their motorbikes, every hour or
so cows might amble across the bog to drink at the waterside, and there was
one never to be forgotten occasion, at Rathangan, when a huge sow threw her
enormous bulk into the water. Apparently the unrelenting heat was too much
for her, so, leaving her family on the bank, she took a dip to cool off – smack in
the middle of my swim – and there was I believing that pigs never took to
water. Still, such happenings are the stuff of fishing in Ireland.

Gradually I got the hang of what Gordon was teaching. It must have taken
me ten bites or more before I saw the sense in scaling down the telltale lift shot
to a No. 6. Grand Canal bream were super-sensitive to one thing, namely any
kind of shot drag. I found that the bream would not take a moving bait; it had

to be absolutely still on the canal bed. I assumed that this was learned behaviour on their part, yet how could that be? Fifteen years ago there were few fish at Ticknevin that had been fished over, much less caught. Yet, even then, it was always rudd or perch that made bold snatches at hookbaits – never the larger bream!

*   *   *   *   *

Bream behaviour depends largely on the depth and type of water in which they live. The Grand Canal varies tremendously in water quality, flow and colour. Back toward Dublin the water was almost gin-clear, with great expanses of lily pads providing cover. Those sections were known rudd and tench habitat. Colour only crept into the water beyond Prosperous, past the village of Allenwood. It was, and still is, generally accepted that canal water needed to be chocolate in colour before it could be classed as holding bream. Such conditions prevail at the stretch where the narrow-gauge railway crosses the canal from the peat bog, en route to the power station.

Another fish-producing swim was where water flows into the canal from a pipe that emerges from the peat briquette plant. There was never much flow, but seemingly enough to create conditions that attracted fish, though rudd always seemed to dominate.

From Ticknevin, onward to Shannon Harbour, the Grand Canal remains a wild, almost natural fishery. The only positive change that I've seen over fifteen years consistent fishing has been the arrival of roach. Some authorities claim that these fish have swum in from the Shannon, crossing the width of Ireland for nearly 80 miles; others insist that pikemen introduced the roach in the years that livebaiting dominated the fishing scene. Either way, the roach are taking over from rudd – which I don't consider a good thing. There are at least three major river systems in Ireland that contain and can support vast shoals of roach, whereas the rudd, that made for traditional sport, are fast disappearing from those waters in which we expect to find them. It is as though roach arrive through one door and rudd depart from another. Perhaps the competition for food and territory is won by the more active species.

One advantage in the arrival of roach on the canal is that they provide winter sport for anglers, something usually missing in a shallow water fishery, rapidly affected by temperature change, where only rudd and bream are the mainstays.

*   *   *   *   *

Our fishing session produced nearly 50 lbs of bream for Dickinson, while I had 20 lbs or so made up of a few bream and a lot of rudd. I hadn't quite got the hang of the bream biting characteristics, something Gordon seemed to detect by a kind of angling witchcraft! I didn't even see half of the bites he had. It was as though he *expected* a bream to be mouthing the bait, rather than knowing it by seeing a registration at the float. Obviously he was totally familiar with his tackle and technique. He never filled the swim in. His groundbaiting was a small, initial feeding before his tackle was set up. Then he waited until fish came before putting anything else into the water. After he had caught a few fish, he would feed golfball-sized lumps, at about ten-minute intervals, with loose-fed maggots thrown before each successive cast.

Hooking a bream produced a rhythm in his tackle handling. The fish was drawn away from its feeding area by a smooth sweep of the rod, lifted to mid-water and fought out within an arc of 20 feet of the net. I never did see Gordon allow a fish to splash on the surface, apart from the last flurry that most fish make when they see the rim of the landing net. He kept the swim peaceful and that, I now know, was his secret for keeping it productive.

*   *   *   *   *

I continued to visit Prosperous regularly, introducing many friends to the fishing. Although we always tended to return to familiar swims, we began to travel around, taking in far more of the canal than I had ever previously fished.

I had a memorable experience on the canal about five years ago during the second week in May. While walking along the bank beyond Ticknevin, where the waterway crosses a huge area of bogland empty of roads, I noticed from a distance that the water surface was agitated. Getting closer, I saw a mass of bubbles bursting up from the bottom, spreading across the water for what seemed at least a 100-yard stretch. The bubbling identified the position of a massive shoal of bream. There must have been thousands, probably concentrated in a spawning frenzy, although the vigorous bubbling display suggested that many were preoccupied with rooting around in the bottom detritus. I doubted whether these fish would take a bait; the specimens occupied with sexual activity certainly wouldn't, and who could blame them?

There was another occasion when the lift-bite and soft-take theory went haywire. John Woods and I arrived in early April to find the canal swept by blustery winds that created waves at least a foot high. Difficult conditions in which to shot a float down carefully! We decided to tackle up with wagglers, carrying a lot of weight, that could ride fairly high in the water, and threw quite an amount of feed into our swims, reckoning that there wasn't much chance of good fishing and that we might stop a few fish in front of us for long enough to get them to feed. There were offers straight away, both from bream and rudd, which made bold bites that slid the floats away purposefully. We could hardly see the bites clearly. Only the strongest pull had any effect as the floats rose and fell on the troubled water. John was hell-bent on changing to a quivertip, although, after some argument, he had to agree that we were probably catching as many fish as the tip might produce by continuing to feed, little but often, while offering three or four maggot-size hookbaits.

Five hours fishing gave us over 100 lbs between us – not easy even in calm conditions. It may well have been that the bream were avidly feeding prior to the arrival of the spawning season, and perhaps that movement of the bait was, in the conditions prevailing, acceptable to them.

Although there had always been a heavy colour to the water at Ticknevin, this seemed to be rapidly increasing. The extra turbidity could not be explained by wave action but must have come from the activity of bream sifting among the loose silt on the canal bed. I have frequently noticed a similar occurrence after a barge or pleasure launch had passed through the swim.

Farther east, toward Dublin, there is a section of the Grand Canal that is noted for its tench. Unused by any form of boat traffic, the canal has large areas of water 'cabbage' and other plantlife. There at Digby Bridge the canal is shallow and only fishes well when the light has left the water, after the sun has dropped below the trees that line the banks.

A ritual grew up during the Prosperous Gala Week. Anglers, fishing the competition, would finish the match, rush back to their various guesthouses for the evening meal and then vie with one another in choosing the first swim on the 'Digby' stretch. The transition from avid match angler to pleasure fisherman was quite astounding. Men who during a match could hardly take their eyes off a float would suddenly relax and start chatting amicably to one another. At first I thought that it was just a matter of getting away from a 'peg' and the tension of individual challenge. Now, after years of evening sessions at Digby Bridge, I am inclined to believe that it is the fish, the tench themselves, that bring about this radical change in their personalities. . . .

CHAPTER SEVENTEEN

A Woman of Mayo

IRELAND

The boat drifted on a rumbustious sea off the north coast of Mayo. We had left Port Turlin, a small hamlet north-east of Belmullet, on a hazy, rainswept morning to seek our fishing close to massive rocks that rise from the seabed. The Stags are one of those Irish sea angling marks that strike more than a wisp of fear into the intrepid angler. Although frightening, I confess the presence of reefs, rocky islands or towering cliffs adds another dimension to my sea fishing. I always feel that I'm in with a chance when the environment suggests danger. Fishing over open ground on a sea that has nothing in sight to the horizon never has quite the same appeal.

The idea of visiting the mark came from Hilda Clinton of Westport, a friend of many years who fishes the Atlantic coast of Ireland throughout the season. Hilda, a staunch member and one-time officer of the Irish Federation of Sea

The Stags, dark granite peaks rising from the sea off the north coast of Mayo. The surrounding seabed is among the best of Ireland's sea angling marks.

Anglers, is a fantastic organizer, a humorous companion and a great angler. Throughout Europe there are hundreds of international sea anglers who have sought her advice and benefited from her experience. She is fortunate to have been born within sight of Clew Bay and the broad Atlantic.

Hilda's plan, on this occasion, was to get some heavy fishing at The Stags, followed by a late afternoon session near into the coast for fleshy dabs and the chance of a specimen gurnard, for which this sea area was famous.

Our sport started well with pollack hitting our baits as soon as they reached the seabed. Hilda was first into fish, which I came to expect whenever I fished with her. I eventually concluded that it was a question of tackle presentation. Hilda believed in heavy gear, claiming, I think rightly, that too many sea anglers practice a light tackle approach to the sport without regard to the particular conditions created by different species, day and place.

Hilda insisted on a positive contact with the seabed, ensuring that the weight and baits sat exactly where fish could find them. This called for a stout rod, 50-lb line and at least a pound sinker. For my part, I used a 20-lb fibreglass wand and nylon which inevitably had a deal of stretch, arguing with Hilda that I experienced a better fight on my choice of tackle. She, in turn, pointed out that I had first to feel the bite, then hook the fish before I could enjoy any fight. Hilda insisted that her terminal gear gave a better indication of a bite and enabled her to hook far more of the offers that came.

It's an argument that will never be settled. I am convinced, however, that the heavy ground tackle does result in more positive hooking, particularly when there are shy-biting species about, as the line transmits tweaks and soft mouthings far better. Furthermore, a lot of fish manage to hook themselves where they have to take a bait against the drag of a heavy sinker. Some will argue that hooking the fish as a result of recognizing a bite is what the sport is about – true, but quite against the principles of uptide fishing!

On this particular day, Hilda caught most in the steep swells that were battering the offshore rocks. We had a super catch, of pollack, coalfish and ling, so decided to motor inshore to find the smaller but, to me, more valuable fish. Our skipper was quite definite about the prospects, predicting that we'd get dabs over mixed ground and gurnards about 50 yards further along the base of the cliffs. So we set out to prove him right.

I felt totally justified in setting up the lightest tackle that I had brought to Mayo; an 8-ft rod with 10-lb line has always been my favourite weapon to use in shallow water. Yet although Hilda had to remain with the deepsea gear, there still wasn't much difference in our respective catch rate. While I assumed the tease-them-onto-the-bait stance, Hilda flung her baited tackle across the gunwale where it sank like a ton of bricks. I couldn't see how she might detect bites from anything as small as a dab, but hook them she did.

I managed one sneaky 'I told you so' laugh at her expense, though admittedly the episode could have had a happier outcome. We were both into

One of Ireland's 'Master Anglers', Hilda Clinton from Westport is
always to be found far out over the deepwater marks and catching the
better fish.

fish and swung them aboard simultaneously. Hilda's dab undoubtedly
bordered on being a specimen and she waved it vigorously toward me, as
though to ram home the point that Women's Lib was clearly in the lead. The
fish leaped out of her hand, flipped off the hook and fell into a gap between
the deck and the hatch that covered the engine. Nobody aboard had any
intention of rooting around in the oily water of the bilge to retrieve her catch –
so I found myself back in the game!

The mark, within a mile of Port Turlin, would have made a superb situation
to fish from the shore, what with clean sand below the boat, in only 30 feet of
water, needing a cast of only 50 yards. The cliffs were very low, only about 30

feet high, and the footing appeared to be perfect. Sad to say, most shore fishermen who visit Ireland's oceanic coastline rarely walk out on to the wilder headlands or tramp to those places that offer real solitude. Thousands of similar shore marks exist along the indented Atlantic coastline, most of them offering fish that cannot be trawled out from the foul ground.

We fished on for dabs, catching the odd small plaice from the same ground. There must have been a nursery for flats below the keel. I'm sure that the area has enormous feed potential for juvenile stocks. Just around the corner from Benwee Head, slightly farther south, there used to be a fishery with a reputation for providing quality rays and flats. That was in Broadhaven Bay and around Blacksod Bay, north of Achill. Unfortunately, it was too easy to net out and doesn't fish like it did in the past.

The skipper kept on about gurnets (gurnards), and the number of near specimen fish that he'd had off his special mark. There may have been an ulterior motive for the species are regarded as one of the best baits for use in lobster pots, and he made his living potting the surrounding vast acres of rocky seabed. We listened, but were content to stay put; after all, it isn't often that one happens on flatfish with the size of the Port Turlin dabs.

Clew Bay and conservation

The bay, below Croagh Patrick, is Hilda Clinton's home patch. Out from the historical town of Westport lie some of the best fishing locations that Ireland can offer the sea angler. If ever there was a case for creating a National Park in saltwater, Clew Bay must be the place. Bounded by Connemara to the south and the Curraun Peninsula to the north, the bay is protected across its Atlantic opening by the bulk of Clare Island which serves to break the worst of the westerly gales. Within the deeply indented bay are shallows and reefs, liberally dotted with hundreds of grass-topped islands.

This is ray and tope country. Westport gained its international reputation for producing enormous common skate, huge torpid monkfish and a variety of lesser members of the shark and skate brigade. During the 1960s and 1970s, because of the safe conditions and quantities of fish, many competitions were held here. The clubhouse built by Hilda and the members of local angling clubs became the meeting place for fishermen from near and afar, and still resounds to a host of different languages.

Clew Bay isn't all shallow ground and safe boating conditions. Off Clare Island there is very deep water and a greater variety of species. Porbeagle and blue shark make their appearance every year while the deeper rocky seabed areas have enormous ling, cod and pollack. Mike Shepley has a photograph (I think it's on the wall of his study) of what remained of a ling that he fought to the surface. The head and a small part of the fish's body weighed well over 10 lbs when it came into his boat. The rest of the body that didn't get

Clew Bay, Co. Mayo, can provide everything for the travelling angler. Calm waters, within the deep bay, and the rough and tumble of the broad Atlantic.

weighed was taken in mid-water by a huge shark. Mike's fight with the ling came to a halt and developed into a tug of war with an unseen common adversary.

If any one fish made Westport's reputation, it had to be the common skate. They were big, prolific and, like the monkfish, reliable. The depth of water in Clew Bay makes it ideal country for the big-fish angler, deep enough to encourage the larger specimens to reside but not to the extent of provoking a fight that cannot be coped with. Skate fishing is a back-breaking exercise. . . .

It was an inspired idea when Westport, its local clubs and the Irish Federation of Sea Anglers designated Clew Bay a conservation area. Realizing that the killing of skate and monkfish could not continue forever without rapidly depleting stocks, the clubs asked all fishermen to return the large fish. Tagging programmes were instituted and I believe that we are now seeing results from the policy. Skate are returning to the sea area and monkfish can again be caught. Competition anglers are awarded so many points for a skate or monkfish boated; then the fish is immediately returned to the water. Weighing is not really vital and a 'Great White Hunter' photograph can always be had as the unhooking takes place.

Fishing for skate is hard on the angler and
his tackle. This fisherman is in real trouble
unless he can get the fish moving, a rod bent
over the gunwale can snap in seconds!

Nobody wants to see fish disappear as potential rod and line sport. Without doubt, the unnecessary killing of skate and other huge fish can have a serious effect on stocks. These species are slow to mature, they inhabit an area in a ratio consistent with the food availability, and they are now under threat from commercial interests. In former times the trawlermen couldn't sell them, so didn't take them. Recently it has become a different story. Practically everything that lands on the harbour wall is saleable! The charter boat skippers of Westport deserve medals for their support of the conservation concept. All of them understand the consequences of overfishing and take great pains to explain to travelling anglers the sound reasoning behind the strategy.

If I had to have only one reason to return to Westport it would be for the sunsets. Bing Crosby made a fortune singing about Galway Bay, but I doubt if the sun going down in that spot is any more heart-moving than the panorama of evening light that silhouettes Clew Bay's islets or rims the peaks of Clare Island.

'Where The Hell is The End of Main?'

CANADA

The first glimpse of Manitoba, from the cockpit of an Air Canada aircraft, destroyed all my illusions about Canada. My school years' geography books had whetted my appetite with spectacular pictures of the Rocky Mountains, but Manitoba was something else. Flat and enormous describes the central prairie lands that stretch for thousands of miles east to west. Here and there I could see huge areas of water and one or two rivers meandering through forest and arable land.

Ches Scofield, a Canadian backwoodsman, wanted everybody to catch fish.

I had arrived at Winnipeg with Mike Shepley to meet Doug Raynbird, who worked with the Manitoba tourism organization filming all kinds of activities within the province. We were here to fish for a variety of North American species. Doug suggested that we start with a trip to the Red River, where it ran through a number of small lakes after leaving the gigantic expanse of Lake Winnipeg.

Distances are hard for a European to define when in Canada. We drove out north from the city on Main Street. Hours later we were still driving, north of Selkirk, on Main Street (Highway 32), although by now it had become a dirt road! Apparently, our destination was a fishing camp at Breezy Point, on the Red River lakes. When we finally arrived, we were met by a jovial, burly man clothed in a tee-shirt carrying the legend, 'Where the Hell is the End of Main?' After our lengthy journey, I can understand why his customers ask the question.

Ches Scofield and his wife Betty catered for all watersport interests but first and foremost he was a fisherman. There were outboard-powered aluminium fishing boats everywhere, one of them destined to be our craft for exploring the hundreds of bays and backwaters that formed the interesting shoreline. Ches's statement that there were even carp to be caught seemed a bit far-fetched until he explained that mid-European immigrants had brought carp fry to Canada thus spreading the species into a number of suitable waters.

This was interesting if only in exploding the myths about carp and winter-kill. In Manitoba, carp are subjected to winter temperatures far below anything experienced in Europe. The ice on the lakes, however shallow, can be 8–12 inches thick each year, in a winter that can last for at least six months! Very few carp are found dead in spring and the fish grow to 30 lbs or more.

Our first fishing outing was to be for sauger, a fish that resembles both the European zander and North American walleye. Although it doesn't grow too large, it is highly prized by local anglers. Our tackle system came as a bit of a shock. The terminal rigs were all of the paternoster variety, formed in wire and carrying long-shank hooks to accommodate the fish baits that are used. There was more than a hint of sea angling about this unsophisticated set-up.

Ches told us to be on the dock in an hour, while he gathered the necessary baitfish. I thought, naturally, that he meant to fish for whatever we were going to use; but no, Ches Scofield was organized. We reached his landing stage while he was still out getting the hookbaits. What we saw, out on the water, can only be described as a fishing dinghy with a tennis court being pushed through the water ahead of it!

He had rigged one of his boats with an open-ended, box-like contraption made of a wood frame covered in chicken wire. As it was pushed through the water, small surface-swimming fish were caught up in the trap. In minutes, Ches had hundreds of tiny, silvery minnow-like fish.

Very similar to the European zander, saugers are regarded as fine fish to eat. They weren't enormous but they certainly fought well, although I thought the tackle was restrictive.

Canadian fishermen believe in horsepower. We took two of the aluminium craft and sped out, travelling like the wind, passing flocks of pelicans and gulls, creaming over the surface to a weeded bay where we could just see a line of current that indicated the passage of the Red River through the lake's breadth. Ches instructed me on the baiting system which consisted of killing the baitfish and passing the long-shank hook through its length so that only the hookpoint emerged below the vent. Then the paternoster, with two or three separate baits, was lowered into only 10 feet of water. I was told to impart a slight jigging movement to the rig; not a sink and draw action but just enough to give the baitfish a quivering motion. I didn't wait long for action. It came as a slight pull, which developed into a lusty thumping as the fish realized that it was hooked. Imagine my surprise when I brought up my first sauger to find that it was only about 12 inches long. Ches showed no emotion at all, remarking that saugers 'aren't very big but they're great fighters!' Here was a sharp difference between the European and Canadian attitudes to fishing. At home we seem to value the specimen fish of a species, whereas our friends across the Atlantic get a lot more fun out of fishing, and catching, their nominated species, evidently going for selectivity rather than size.

This notion was reinforced next day when a friend of Doug's, Bill Burdeney, a newspaperman from Winnipeg, arrived to show us how to catch carp. His methods were an even greater shock. Bill believed in jigging for his fish. None of your groundbaiting, fishing legered cereal baits, boilies or bite-indicators for him. His favourite fish were the carp and he proceeded to show us all how stupid they can be.

The tackle system was so simple. A short, spinning-type rod, fixed-spool and 10-lb line to a weighted hook on which Bill wound a type of earthworm. These jigheads are nowadays used in Britain by sea anglers to present plastic baits like the 'Mr Twister' for pollack and cod.

Bill dropped the bait to the bed of the lake and proceeded to 'bounce' the rod tip up and down. Five minutes of this and he had his first carp on and fighting. It was a beautiful common of 10 lbs. My faith in years of systematic carping, using all the new-fangled nonsense with which the European carp angler is bombarded, evaporated! Bill had done it by bobbing a worm up and down on the hard lakebed, and he promptly showed us all how to repeat the technique. We had another carp and another before the spell was broken by the arrival of a silver, perch-like species that was promptly named white bass. Burdeney explained that not everybody 'fished' for carp; some impatient 'sporting' characters had the massive gall to hunt for them with a bow and arrow – hardly, I thought, the tactics for Redmire.

Bill told us stories of his winter fishing; hauling a hut out on to the ice, complete with a pot-bellied stove inside to provide an ideal barrier against the weather. The lads sat round inside fishing through holes in the ice that they bored with an auger. He agreed that the carp weren't silly enough to be caught in the depth of winter but most of the other species could be taken. I got the impression that this sort of activity was also an opportunity to share a yarn or two over the odd drink or more! Still, that's fishing. . . .

Safari to George Lake

What I would have given for a full tin of worms was the thought that came to me as I fought a flashy bass back to the boat's side. Doug Raynbird had brought us by light aircraft to George Lake, hidden away in thick conifer forests in eastern Manitoba, promising we would find masses of small-mouth black bass. The lake held the record for the species, all caught over rocky shoals that lay just beneath the surface of the water, visible from the air as our floatplane skimmed the tops of the trees to land in a flurry of spray.

The backwoods of Canada are served by a fantastic variety of amphibious aircraft. The pilots of the floatplanes that drop anglers and hunters into the wilderness are prepared to carry things of practically any shape or size. I saw planes flying over the woods with iron bedsteads, sheets of hardboard, aluminium boats and piles of domestic gear attached outside to the sponsons. So fishermen and their tackle present no problem!

Our tackle boxes were stuffed with spinning lures, though I had a few worms in a can, saved from the carping venture. I wanted to give the bass a try on my matchrod, using float tackle. Doug and I shared a dinghy to fish over the rocky reef. We could see the boulders, reputedly as big as houses, clearly in the water; they were only a foot below the surface and were completely free of weed. Doug started to spin with a Mepps No.1, while I went for an antenna float with a small worm on the hook.

Twenty seconds was all the time I had to wait. A tremble of the float and the fish was off with a rush, giving me one of the best fights that I've ever enjoyed on a 13-footer. Bass do not give up easily. Although closely resembling a European perch, their fight is totally different. The fish move faster, making a rapid series of runs both deep and at the surface. The way they turned and skidded off at right angles was amazing. I made many mistakes when landing them; assuming that a fish was tired and ready for the net, I was caught too often with my net arm at full stretch and a fish that tore line off the spool.

While I built a catch of bass, Doug was steadily producing fish on the spinning lure, even though it tended to get hung up on hidden underwater rocks as he sought a pathway through the boulders. Float tackle allowed me to drop the bait into spaces between the rocks. This area of the lake was alive with fish over the reefs. Looking a little like a European perch, the small-mouth black bass is a splendid fellow – green marbled flanks with dark blotchings. (See frontispiece.) We fished until it was dark, and then headed for the comfort of a genuine log cabin, built on a grassy knoll above the lake. We didn't venture inside immediately, for there was a sunset of such magnificence that we could only rush for the cameras.

As full night fell, the forest came alive with sounds of the wilderness. Chipmunks chattered among the branches and an occasional deep braying sound told us that there were bears among the thickets. Whether fear sharpens the hearing of the town dweller, I don't know. Sufficient to say that in no time at all I became aware of every tiny sound that cut the stillness of the night. Mike, meantime, wrestled with his wood-burning stove to produce a magnificent beef hash.

Over the years, visitors to George Lake and its cabin had faithfully recorded their catches in a huge book. Among the stories of fish that got away and others that weren't so fortunate, there were countless mentions of 'lakers', a reference to the lake trout *Salvelinus namaycush*, actually a member of the char group. These always appeared to be caught deep down in the open water of

our lake, at 90 feet or thereabouts. Doug told me that there were times, especially at spawning, when the lake trout came into shallower areas, seeking gravelly streams entering the lake, but that it was definitely a deepwater species. The local anglers had developed downrigger systems for trolling a large spoon, not too successfully in terms of fish landed but sufficiently so to make them interesting.

I asked Doug what he thought about offering a dead bait, fished down on the bottom, and he replied that some anglers did, in fact, troll a mounted deadbait, and caught. It took me quite a time to get the message across that I was thinking in terms of simulating our method of deadbaiting for pike or legering a fishbait in the sea. Doug could be forgiven for his scepticism as he always used spinners and lived at least 2000 miles from saltwater!

In the morning I made up both of my specimen pike rods with a 2-ounce sinker carrying a single-hook running trace. We mounted a sort of whitefish, said to be a smelt, on each rig and spent several minutes lowering them to the bottom. During this time the boat drifted slowly before the wind, which

Everywhere on the plains of Manitoba there are rivers and lakes . . . enough for everybody. The place is crowded if one meets another sportfisher during a day's fishing.

meant that the baits would drag across the bottom. Possibly in the course of this they might raise a cloud of sand or whatever made up the bed of the lake. We soon found out that the lakebed was littered with rocks, for the baits made momentary halts, pulling the rod tips over into the water.

Ten-pound line has a hell of a lot of stretch in it when over 90 feet is off the spool. Doug and I grew accustomed to the flexing of the rod tips and tautness of line as we drifted very slowly. I didn't notice any sudden pull or nodding to my rod nor could I feel pressure on the rod itself; all that happened was that the line angle changed. Thinking I was snagged, I wound in a few yards. The rod went over in a lusty bend and stayed bent. There was no thumping or discernible pulling. Depth obviously smoothed out the fish's activities.

I started to pump carefully, getting back 4–5 yards of nylon before I felt the trout. Then I really knew that I was in business. The fish might have lifted in the water because it made a sudden dash for the bottom, taking the rod tip below the water's surface where it bent round the hard chine of the boat. My rod might be absolutely right for playing large pike but it didn't have much

Lake trout from George Lake, Manitoba. This member of the char
family is found in very deep water; mine was hooked and raised from a
little over 90 feet.

effect on that lake trout. For the time being it was stalemate. I suppose the
depth and pressure of water defeated the power of the rod blank.

It took me ten minutes at least to get the fish moving, and even then I could
only recover a few turns of line to the reel. My line remained stretched tight;
something had to give, and it proved to be the fish. It came up slowly and
heavily, without any of the battling characteristics normally associated with
the trout family. Eventually it lay finning on the surface – a dull, liberally
spotted, silvery fish, deep and powerful in body with a small head – still
moving purposefully as though little affected by the pressure change. Over
went the net and I brought the first of our lakers into the boat. We weighed it
at just over 9 lbs.

Two hours went by before the next bite came. It was Doug's turn to hit a
rather bigger fish which took the bait and fought to exactly the same pattern –
nothing flamboyant, just a ponderous weight on the line. After the hook was
released, this laker went back over the side and tore down into the pitch-black
water.

Doug suggested a shore lunch, as he needed additional film footage, to
which I immediately agreed. His display of Canadian backwoodscraft was a
delight to watch and share. We had landed on a huge slab of rock, well away
from the dense thickets that fringed most of the lake. There is always evidence

A ritual among Canadian gamefishers . . . the shore lunch provides
ideal cut-away shots for Doug's camera. Fireplaces are carefully
constructed on rock shelves, far from the lakeside trees.

in the bush of earlier campfires as the Canadian anglers have a rigid code of
conduct, no fires being built where they could become a hazard to the forest.
Doug's backpack contained the necessary ingredients for our meal: a huge,
blackened frying pan, a slab of lard and simple tin plates. Sizzling trout fillets
gave off a delicious aroma that must have drifted across the water to where
Mike Shepley was fishing, for within minutes, displaying the look of a hungry
man, he brought his boat skimming in to our landing place. Mike had another
trout, taken on a spoon which he had fished deep off a rocky reef in the middle
of the lake. His fight had been different. The spoonbait had almost been
wrenched off the line as it fluttered in mid-water. I suppose that the trout took
his lure as a live fish, so made a spirited attack, whereas our deadbaits were
picked up in no particular hurry.

Canada teased me with its fishing – so many species and so many waters. I
doubt if there is such a thing as a crowded fishery!

CHAPTER NINETEEN

The Cod of Stonehaven

SCOTLAND

Scotland has a reputation for commercial landings of all kinds of demersal fish. I have been told, by Joyce West who is a journalist involved with the commercial fishing industry, that Scotland is now responsible for at least two-thirds of the fish we eat in Britain. Everybody knows of such famous ports as Peterhead, Arbroath and Aberdeen but I had one of my greatest sea angling experiences from the tiny east-coast port of Stonehaven.

Over a period of several years trawlers had been losing nets to wreckage on the seabed only a few miles from the harbour. Accurate echo sounding, with video graph recorders, had shown that the problems were being caused by three main hulks; the commercial fishermen figuring that the wrecks presented the opportunity for a better catch than was offered by the open ground. Much larger cod used the shelter of the wrecks and finished up in the cod-end when the trawl was dragged, with any accuracy, alongside the underwater obstructions. Unfortunately, some of the trawlers had fished a bit too close to the larder!

Local small boat skipper Raymond Cargill realized that the wrecks were ideal sites for rod and line angling, particularly as the Gantocks had faded as a noted mark among Scottish sea anglers. Learning of his efforts and the quality of fish that were coming to his boat *Andara*, we arranged a trip to coincide with the making of a new film for the Scottish Tourist Board.

An invitation to fish a virgin wreck, thought never previously to have seen a rod and line, is a rare opportunity, and I jumped at the chance when I received a telephone call suggesting that the tides were right for wrecking and that the film ought to make space for the cod off Stonehaven.

Apparently there are three known wrecks lying near due east of the port. Two of them had, at that time, provided good catches with fish up to 33 lbs; the third was not thought attractive as it lay closer inshore. None of the wrecks was large but they sat on a clean sandy seabed, probably representing the only obstruction in the area. As such, they would provide conditions for plantlife to flourish, offer hiding places to invertebrate animals and protect resident fish from the full pressure of the tides. The security and improved feeding opportunities made them natural assembly points.

The call to travel to Scotland came at a time when I was experimenting with

Laid out on the Stonehaven harbour wall, our catch of superb cod, though many more, full of roe, were returned to the sea to spawn and provide future sport.

artificial lures for boat fishing, not only pirks but a wide variety of plastic and rubber baits active enough to attract the predatory instincts of most sea species. Many sea anglers like using pirks, as they have in-built weight to carry the bait down fast, though I find they near kill your arms and back muscles after hours of lowering and sharply raising the rod tip. West of England wreck fishers had switched to using two or three rubber sandeels on a nylon paternoster rig, for round fish, whenever the tide curtailed their conger-fishing activities.

I had been playing around with wriggly, plastic lures called 'Mr Twisters', which had tremendous action but of course no weight to get them down in the water. I started by fishing these lures on a simple nylon paternoster, each of them mounted with a 6/o hook driven through the plastic body; but the baits spun so rapidly that they completely tangled the hook snoods. What I needed was jigheads, something like American anglers use when casting soft lures to bass.

I began the Twister era casting a variety of differently sized jig weights, inserting a long-shanked hook in the casting mould before the lead was poured. They gave immediate trouble when I took them out to fish over rough ground, for the free hookpoint would snag up on any weed or wreckage on the seabed.

Then came a breakthrough when a complete set of jigheads was sent to me from America. They all had an offset to the eye of the hook, on which the line was tied, so that the hookpoint 'swam' in an upright fashion (the bait appearing to fish on its back). Coincidentally, a friend from the west coast of

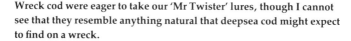

Wreck cod were eager to take our 'Mr Twister' lures, though I cannot see that they resemble anything natural that deepsea cod might expect to find on a wreck.

Scotland, Jim MacLanaghan, gave me some of his weights. He had lost a lot of normal rigs pollack fishing in the Firth of Clyde, a rocky area with extensive weedbeds. So he had set about adapting ordinary 5- and 6-ounce casting leads with the nylon attachment ring offset in the American manner. Now he was enjoying enormous success with his lures while competition fishing in his offshore waters.

Back I went to modifying my own casting moulds so that the bend of the hook could be cast into the weights with the hook eye coming out of the weight on the same side as the hookpoint and barb. The lures then swam with the point uppermost, so no more problems of catching up in weed. Losses were reduced to practically nothing!

I went to Scotland with all the jigheads and Twisters that I could muster, along with a few lugworms and pirks as insurance – just in case my ideas were wrong.

I liked Stonehaven immediately. The harbour was quiet yet there was an air of efficiency about the place. The boats lying alongside the wall were clean and well cared for, as is customary along the Scottish east coast. *Andara* was almost clinical in appearance and her skipper proved to be superbly knowledgeable about his 'patch'.

When we motored out from the harbour on the first morning, we got a shock. A trawler was lying, motionless, close to the estimated position of our first wreck. We learned later that it had been too close to the wreck with its nets, fouling the gear below on the seabed. The crew could be seen working feverishly to mend the nets and attach new bobbins to the footropes.

Our skipper pinpointed the wreck on his sounder, so we found it easily. *Andara*'s paper trace indicated that there was a lot of loose debris strewn around, and a whole parcel of fish swimming above the hulk. Having made up our rods on the way out, we lost no time in getting them over the side. We began a drift that Raymond said would carry us along the length of the wreck. Mike Shepley, as usual, had the first pull from a sizeable fish. He played it carefully up to the boat to show us our first cod from the newly found fishing mark.

I started purposefully with a choice of two baits; a pirk on the bottom of the rig to give sufficient weight and one Twister, tied in on a boom about 3 feet above the heavy metal. Soon one of the lures was grabbed. A heavy thumping motion, lasting for a couple of seconds, indicated the presence of a cod. Then the fish resisted the power of the rod by diving back down toward the wreck. It jerked around savagely, but with steady pumping I got it moving upward. When it eventually arrived at the surface I found myself with the first Scottish cod of over 20 lbs that I had ever taken. But it wasn't on the Twister lure; the pirk had proved a greater temptation. With some trepidation, I removed the heavy pirk and replaced it with one of my own jigheads.

It took me only a few minutes to change the rig and lures but meanwhile both Mike and Ian Dunne, another of Scotland's international anglers, had hooked into large cod. There was no way that I could lower my gear again as they were both screaming for a gaff, which meant spending the next five minutes helping to boat two huge fish, both of them over 25 lbs.

With the panic over, I was just able to get my lures down when Raymond yelled 'Lines up!' We had reached the end of the wreck and he was ready to motor uptide to begin another fruitful drift. Nobody argues with the skipper on charter boats, so I had the pleasure of winding up lures that hadn't been given a chance to fish!

Our second drift began quietly. The skipper commented that the tide was a little stronger, which would take the boat at an angle right across the centre of the wreck. He watched the echo sounder trace eagerly as the shape of the underwater hulk began to appear on the trace. 'Right, down you go,' was the cry from the wheelhouse, and we let the rigs go together. Within seconds Ian shouted 'Fish on,' and then Mike gave a roar as his rod bent into another heavy fish. Just my luck to get nothing, I thought – then it happened. Wham! Over went the tip and a tremendous strain began tearing at my arms. Feeling every thump of the fish via the line, I could almost see it shaking its great craggy head from side to side. Slowly it began moving uptide, obviously intent on regaining the shadow of the wreck. Setting the slipping clutch to a

This cod chose the metal jig rather than the paternostered 'Twister' lure. It may be that the pirk gives off both flashes of reflected light and vibrations.

Twenty-eight pounds of fleshy, prime cod from a Stonehaven wreck produced only a smile from our skipper – inferring he had seen many larger fish!

position where I knew that a really heavy fish could take line, without causing a breakage, I gave it some stick. It was fantastic fishing, for we had all chosen lightish rods, with lines of 20-lb to allow the maximum sport from fish taking the artificial lures.

My fish gave me a hell of a battle, taking line repeatedly. Gradually, I began getting some nylon back on to the spool. There was little possibility of my pumping the fish; I just had to wind very slowly, keeping up a steady pressure on the cod, always with a bend in the rod. On the way to the surface my fish changed direction, always dangerous on light tackle because the force of the flowing tide is added to the weight and strength of the cod.

Finally I had some luck. The fish turned back, with little pressure from me, and rose in the water to lie on its side within reach of Mike's gaff. It weighed 28 lbs, and I was delighted to see that the Twister was neatly hooked into its upper jaw – a success for the artificial lure.

We continued to catch cod after cod, and eventually decided, keeping ten or so, to put the rest back into the sea, since many had not spawned and were full of roe. The released fish didn't appear to have suffered from being hooked and hauled to the surface, giving a flick of the tail to swim down into the murky depths.

The fish on this wreck fed through the tide and then lay quiet as slack water came, suggesting that the small species hunted by the large cod abandon the wreck when conditions allow them to move out over the open ground to feed.

Raymond suggested we leave, as he wanted us to have an hour on another, smaller hulk that lay closer inshore toward Stonehaven.

We found the new mark surrounded by small codling and pollack, swimming high over the superstructure. Pollack can be guaranteed to grab at artificial lures, particularly if there is a definite 'fishy' action. In this shallower water, I didn't mount my Twisters on a sink-and-draw rig, preferring to drift the lure, mounted on a small jighead, downtide.

There was considerably less tide over this wreck, with much less drift on the boat. Luckily, conditions allowed me to stream a long line and trace back to the fish. Whereas cod take the lure and then hold it solidly against the curve of the rod, pollack grab, turn down and dive for the bottom or into the wreck. They are much faster swimmers, well able to break a line if the angler's attention is not riveted to his rod tip.

Our conclusion was that the Twister was well suited to relatively clear water conditions since it is a lure that needs to be seen by fish, whether cod or pollack. Recently, too, I have used the Twister more and more as a shore-casting lure. Fitted with a suitable weight of jighead, it becomes an ideal fish-taker from a rocky coast, where there is deepwater close in to angler's pitch. I find the combination far more effective than conventional spinning lures, which are never heavy enough to achieve the desired casting distance or sinking characteristics.

I have bought these flexible lures in a variety of colours but I am convinced that red is the best attractor for all members of the cod family. Jigheads can be painted (mine are also red) but I don't think that there is any real justification for this. More often than not, I have run out of red jigheads when the better specimens arrive, forcing me to use those direct from the moulds. These bright lead jigs are taken by most predatory round fish just as readily over the wrecks or from the coastline.

CHAPTER TWENTY

Bream among the Windsurfers

HOLLAND

It is the nature of anglers to assume that their chosen sport must have priority anywhere – a claim vigorously contested by other water users. Open any angling journal and you are confronted with the endless argument about the rights of anglers, canoeists, windsurfers and bird watchers. Rarely will you find agreement on how to share the water surface. Yet across the North Sea, in Holland, I found an entirely different attitude; anglers existing alongside boatsmen and windsurfers, none of whom lost their tempers if interests clashed!

A few years ago I had my first chance to fish in Friesland, a north-western province of Holland that rivals the Norfolk Broads or the Lake District in the amount of water available to all manner of sportsmen. Since then I have taken to fishing the lakes and channels of the area whenever I can. Without doubt, this corner of Holland has the best bream fishing anywhere in Europe, and I like to fish there regularly throughout the spring and summer.

The Friesland lakes, or meers, are shallow waters with a high turbidity. Linking canals and wider channels allow the passage of fairly large working boats, of a few hundred tons lading, to deliver raw materials to the factories of Holland's northern towns. These craft use the waterways throughout the year, although in really cold winters both the connecting canals and the lakes are frozen solid.

Friesland has far less arable farming than other areas of the country. Cattle and sheep predominate, and only the latter are seen in the winter months, all dairy cattle being housed from November through to April or May. This type of farming has a tranquillizing effect on the fishing. Practically no pesticides are used on the water meadows, so there is little dangerous residue to enter the water. Despite the fact that animal manure is spread in autumn over huge tracts of grassland, very little appears to leach into the fisheries, although its effect on the flocks of wildfowl that arrive annually from the frozen wastes of Siberia and Spitzbergen cannot be pleasant. A further protection from over-use of Friesland water resources is the natural winter, which is a clearly

Sneekermeer, in the northern province of Friesland, has thousands of quiet backwaters, connecting channels and deep pools where the angler can ply his sport.

defined period when there are no pleasure boats, no windsurfers and no anglers – just the migratory water birds. With a real period of rest, the various waters produce a quality and quantity of fish that is hard to surpass anywhere in Europe.

The waters of Friesland are of the same origin as those of the Norfolk Broads: worked out fuel pits of the Middle Ages which provided peat in a layer up to 6 feet deep. The depth, combined with sunlight penetration and fertility, ensures that there is a vast growth of vegetation to support the invertebrate life on which the fish feed. Some of the waters are on a land mass that was reclaimed from the sea within the last few hundred years. Lakebeds are made up of extremely fertile soil, literally smothered in sea shells which provide a lime content that promotes plant growth.

*   *   *   *   *

A first visit to any fishery always leaves the deepest impression on my mind. In this case my job was to find a new location, different yet close enough, geographically, to Britain to encourage anglers to give it a try. Living at that time in East Anglia, it was natural that I should look at Harwich as a port of exit and toward Holland, our nearest European neighbour. I gathered together a few friends for the trip and we decided to use a watersport centre on Sneekermeer as our base. De Potten was advertised as a recreational centre with bungalow accommodation by the waterside. We arrived to find swims within 20 feet of the front door, and one of our party, Russ Russell, never walked more than twice that distance to fish throughout his stay!

We had a simple choice; either to fish from a boat among the smaller waterways or from the bank. Oddly enough, I like to use a boat, whereas most anglers crave more to 'set their stall out' on *terra firma*. Trevor King, Freddie Tamplin and Russ chose the banks of the nearest lake, within spitting distance of our bungalows, while I set off to a smaller, connected lake that promised less waterborne activity. Nowhere was the depth more than 5 feet. Earlier discussion with Jaap van Riesen, director at the centre, suggested that the bottom of most Friese meers is fairly soft, about 6 inches of ooze over the hard peat bed. Floatfishing was thus far more effective than legering, particularly as there was no need to fish at long range. Bream appeared right under the rod tips. I think that constant boat activity, whether from small craft or the larger work vessels, conditions Dutch fish to move into the banksides without paying much heed to the vibrations set up by anglers.

The first morning's fishing resulted in about 50 lbs of bream to each rod, not to mention the odd roach and rudd among the catch. Quality silver bream, of 2 lbs or more, seemed to share the water almost equally with the larger commons. We each had several gallons of maggots as our main bait and an enormous quantity of groundbait manufactured by Freddie Tamplin in

A marvellous accompaniment to winter leger fishing, migrating
white-front geese arriving from Siberia. If only we anglers could
follow these birds back to their summer paradise of fish and fishing.

'Russ' Russell with an average size bream from De Potten. Out in
the larger, deeper meres there are shoals with fish weighing well
over 10 lbs.

Birmingham along with a variety of new-fangled, though effective, additives.

In the afternoon of the first day I stayed on the bank with the lads. The
fearlessness of the bream shoals was twice demonstrated to us all. During the
after-lunch setting up, Fred decided to bait our various swims afresh. I didn't
notice his arrival behind me as I had a bream on and was concentrating on
playing the fish out. Fred, with his own brand of humour, had built an
enormous ball of feed, about the size of a melon, which he lobbed over my
head to hit the surface about 5 yards out. Not expecting the bomb, I nearly fell
off my box, then launched into a tirade about filling the swim in and finishing
it off for the afternoon. Casting out again, I found that nothing of the sort had
happened. The bream fed, if anything, more voraciously than before!

There were some windsurfers out on the lake with the inevitable beginners among them. Now and then one of the tyros would drift toward my pitch, unable to control the direction without a lot of twisting and turning to cut into the wind. I had another fish on and was lifting it away from the shoal when an unfortunate surfer came straight at me and promptly fell off his board right into the middle of the baited area. I brought the bream in and netted it, swearing under my breath as I watched the poor lad's efforts to clamber aboard the plank. As soon as he drifted off, I lobbed the tackle back where he had fallen and the double-maggot bait went straight into another open mouth. Nothing that happened on or under the water made any difference to the feeding bream; roach and rudd seemed to be wary of noise or splashing but they, too, came back to the feed within minutes of any disturbance. We totalled about another 50 lbs or so each for the afternoon, although Russ, from his bungalow swim, beat us out of sight with two keepnets filling all the time. Jaap van Riesen had described the lake as about 4–5 feet deep with a 6-inch layer of soft ooze. We modified that to the silt layer and 2 feet of bream covered by 2 feet of water!

Day two followed the same pattern: bream and more bream, all coming to a variety of maggot-hookbait combinations. Occasionally one or other of us would try a bunch of worms on the off-chance that a bigger specimen might select the larger juicier bait, but it made little difference to the size of fish hooked. The shoal was immense and seemed to comprise fish all of the same weight. Now and then something more than 3–4 lbs happened along, although 2–3 lbs seemed to be the average weight for the fish.

We moved in the afternoon to a pitch offering deeper water in the channel between Sneekermeer and the town of Sneek. I suppose the water is about 200 yards across, with a buoyed centre channel indicating the fairway for the boat traffic. The bottom ran out as a sloping shelf for about 10 yards and then fell away quite sharply into the deeper cut. The edge of the shelf could be felt easily when plumbing for depth or dragging back a feeder. Some of us altered the gear to fish on the lead.

Immediately the bites were stronger and we had one or two much larger bream, of about 5½ lbs. As a mass of line bites followed, I found myself false striking every couple of minutes until I could settle into a pattern of only hitting the pulls that yanked the quivertip round and kept it bending.

There was nothing sophisticated about the terminal rig or the way in which fish took our offerings; 4-lb line, straight through, seemed right to a size 12 hook. Three maggots with an occasional snippet of lobworm served as the bait with regular, reasonably loose, balls of Freddie's feed to get down in the creeping current.

I used fairly heavy groundbait laced with maggot. The loose-feeding was kept up by filling a feeder with a mixture of maggot and wetted brown crumb. Fish went mad for four hours in the heat of the afternoon and under a sweltering sun I think all the 'rules' of bream fishing were rewritten!

Waiting for his dinner? A Friesland farm cat accompanies me on a
winter spinning expedition as I fish the water alongside a commercial
fisherman's eel trap.

Pulling bream after bream into a waiting net, however, is something I
cannot do for very long. Eventually my interest fails and I have to be off to
pastures new. I had taken a look at a small bay, way off the main channel,
where thick reedmace fringed almost the half circle. It looked perchy to me, so
I stuffed everything into my boat and left the others to their legering. Of
course, the one thing that every angler, who is a member of a party, needs to
check on is whether he has his own bait. I arrived about 50 yards downstream
and across the bay from where the rest of the lads were pitched, set up and
then realized that I had very little to feed to the fish. Fortunately another of
angling's gentlemen was among the larger group. John Burton from Essex, in
response to my shouts of woe, immediately stripped down to his underpants

and swam the bait across to me. Lord knows what the boating fraternity made of a lad breast-stroking across Sneekermeer in the brilliant sunshine, pushing a plastic gallon box ahead of him. Mad dogs and Englishmen?

I didn't get among perch, although roach made the move worthwhile. They patrolled in front of me for most of the late afternoon, with shoals nosing to the surface between the boat and the reeds. They seemed to be feeding on buzzers that clouded the stillwater inside the bay. It occurred to me that a fly rod might be a useful addition, in the future, to the holdall, for the surface feeding from a huge shoal of fish was intense.

One strange thing happened in the cool of an evening on De Potten. Trevor King and I decided to join our Dutch companion anglers in fishing for a pike. Despite the murkiness of the water, there are a lot of men who fish only pike and zander in the lakes. Fishing in England and Ireland, I like to troll a spoon along the edges of reeded banks, so we both put up a light spinning rod with a Norwich spoon and set the baits to follow the boat at about 40 yards distance. Ten minutes quiet rowing brought us into a wide channel, with hard grassy banks, devoid of any waterweed. Then it happened. A sudden wallop to the tip of my rod, which I grabbed and tightened to feel a plunging fish. This was no dour fight, more the sharp pull of a smaller fish attempting to get free. I sensed, after a minute or so playing the fish, that it was no pike; and our first glimpse of the hooked, slab-sided lump proved me right. I had a bronze bream of about 3 lbs cleanly hooked on all three prongs of a treble – opportunist feeding indeed.

How that fish saw the bait in such dark water is difficult to imagine. Perhaps it struck only because that particular bait flutters and vibrates well; the Norwich pattern of spoon, made to resemble a small rudd, is a proven pike taker. One would never suggest such a bait for bream but you never know; even among fish there is always a fool!

Opportunist Angling

THE ARABIAN GULF

A few years ago I had an assignment in the Middle East. I went in company with film producer Michael Shepley, a Scottish international sea angler from Edinburgh, to film the installation of a new gas-drilling rig in a position about 30 miles off the coast of the United Arab Emirates, far out in the Arabian Gulf. What with my sound recording gear and a mass of other technical apparatus, I had no space to include even the basics of sea-angling tackle in my travel kit; a great pity, because the waters around our destination, Dubai, abound in all manner of superb fighting species.

From a helicopter (a somewhat expensive but highly recommendable fish-spotting platform) we sighted the rig being towed by tugs down the Gulf, in a calm sea broken everywhere by clouds of small fish leaping out above the surface of the water. As we flew at 500 feet it was obvious to us that there were many large predators below the visible shoals of smaller fish. Sailfish were our first choice, although there are many shark species as well as oceanic members of the tunny family present in those seas.

I was quite amazed at the view from the helicopter cockpit. The sea was perfectly blue and clear with just occasional darker patches, where light clouds cast a slight shadow. Even tiny flying fish could be easily detected as they broke surface and skittered many yards across the sea. Larger fish appeared as dark, shadowy shapes, moving slowly under the brilliantly lit wavelets.

We landed twenty minutes later on an established working platform, farther south toward the Straits of Hormuz, and had the chance to talk to the guys who spend a large part of their lives far out in the Gulf and similar waters around the globe. They said that during the months spent offshore they had all seen many different fish species, some of a size that defied description.

From their exciting revelations Mike and I gained the impression that this part of the world was rich both in fossil fuels and big-game fishing opportunities. What a place to work in!

Before being taken off the platform to a supply vessel, to begin our filming, we explored the rig, clambering down to the lowest latticework platform 100 feet below the drilling deck. It was getting dark but the powerful lights, strung around the periphery of the rig, splayed a strong blue light that clearly illuminated the sea's surface for 50 feet around the base of each caisson.

It is hard to hear the surface activity of fish when on a production rig because the surrounding noise level is horrific, what with generators whining and massive gear wheels constantly grinding as they combine to spin the drilling pipe from the wellhead, but we could at least see a lot of fish moving in the light shed from the platform. They sped into the ring of illumination, then tore away to the outer darkness in pursuit of small fry.

Mike, who is always on the alert for the chance of some fishing time, had borrowed simple fishing tackle from the rig's cook, who apparently spent some of his off-duty hours dangling a bait in 90 feet of water. Although the kit included some Swedish spinning lures, there were no sinkers, an omission that gave Mike a hell of a task in attempting to cast the light metal spoons. However, he did manage to get a lure cast 20 yards or so toward the main body of swirling fish. On the retrieve a number of shadowy shapes followed the bait almost to the platform steps. We thought that they were huge mullet until one leaped clear out of the water, and we realized that below our feet was the finest shoal of the largest garfish that either of us had ever seen. The fish seemed upwards of 4 feet in length, with bodies that must have measured 6 in across!

The lure was constantly cast but not positively taken. So Mike switched his attack by putting on to the treble hook a sliver of fish bait, again provided by the rig's thoughtful cook. Instantly the garfish changed their tactics, swimming swiftly in, grabbing and hanging on to the bait with long bills.

Mike's first real strike produced a clean hook as the fish had only held the bait, the iron being nowhere near to its mouth. But patience prevailed and soon he hooked the first of his fish. A tremendous fight ensued as the garfish

The head of a huge garfish, its jaw a mass of sharp teeth. The species favours the area around the rigs, lit up at night, where small fish gather to feed.

hurtled off, leaping and cartwheeling across the heads of the shoal. There was little chance of keeping a tight line as the fish changed direction every second or so. It was at least five minutes before it quietened and Shepley was able to swing it up on to the steel grating that formed our foothold.

Four feet long is no exaggeration! It was the largest, fattest garfish that either of us had seen. Mike went on to catch another four from the shoal before they finally left us and headed away from the lighted surroundings. These fish were to be the key to an angling adventure.

Later that night we were swung out and down 200 feet, clinging desperately to the outside of a flimsy ropework cage, on to the deck of the supply boat. The ship was to be our camera platform when, in the early dawn, we headed to meet the rig coming down the Gulf.

After getting the cameras and sound gear stowed, our skipper steamed the boat off a short distance to anchor for a few hours before the working day began. Lounging in his wheelhouse, we read on the sounder that at this predetermined anchorage there was just over 50 feet of water below the keel. The ship was stopped and the Filipino crew got their heads down. We tried to rest but a temperature of over 100 degrees and associated Gulf humidity of 90 per cent isn't conducive to sleeping! So we took a look around the silent ship, and there they were – half a dozen handlines, lying on the aft deck and obviously used by the crew to provide a change in their shipboard diet.

Mike was into fishing immediately. He began by cutting up the largest of the garfish, which we had brought with us to photograph when daylight came. Our first shock came when the sinkers didn't reach bottom. We Europeans are conditioned to fishing the seabed, whereas Asiatic anglers spend most of their time using a baited hook that dangles around in mid-water. So we just had to fish at that depth.

Almost immediately we both experienced sucking bites that tore the rough lines through our fingers. An instant retrieve, although it wasn't easy to see what was coming up from the depths in the light of small deck lamps, confirmed our guess: there was nothing on the lines, neither baits, hooks nor sinkers. Whatever had attacked our baited hooks hadn't stopped to mouth the cut-up fish or inspect the offerings; it was wham and then away! Optimistically, we tied on new hooks, baited them and dropped down again – to be met with an instant repeat performance.

'This is bloody ridiculous,' roared Mike. 'We'll never see a fish on the boat with these lines!' So off he mooched around the deck looking for heavier gear. Eventually he found some incredibly strong nylon line that appeared to be upwards of a couple of hundred pounds breaking strain. Attaching the largest hook on the boat to a shortish piece of wire, we dropped another, much larger bait over the side. Wisely, as it turned out, we fastened the line around one of the ship's bollards and Mike sat on the gunwale with his hand caressing the flowing nylon.

This time things didn't happen immediately. As he sat there patiently, I relaxed, in the frightful heat and humidity, on a coil of rope. After some twenty minutes a tremendous shriek pulled me back to consciousness. Stumbling across the shadowy, cluttered deck I took a hand to the tight nylon, which had jerked out as tightly as a bowstring, to feel the enormous power of something swimming down below the boat.

Pulling together on the nylon handline, we retreated a few yards back on to the deck, when it was suddenly ripped away back across the gunwale. 'Thank the Lord,' I thought, 'we fastened the end around the bollard!' We tugged, gained line for a while and lost it again for more than twenty minutes. Then came the first sign that we could just be winning, and it struck us forcibly that we might need assistance. Our repeated shouts brought a sleepy-eyed crewman tumbling up to see the fun. He had no idea what was going on and, in his eagerness to help, kept putting his bare feet into the coils of line that we had dragged back on to the deck. I had visions of him disappearing at a great rate of knots for the seabed, but fortunately Mike screamed out some choice Scottish curses that soon got through to the lad.

Meanwhile we had seen nothing of the fish. Its species and size were a mystery, but not so the power it possessed. I managed, by hand signals and pidgin English, to get the message across to the Filipino sailor that we needed a length of fine rope – quick! He vanished below decks to arrive back in a flash with a length of plaited stuff perfect for fashioning a tailing rope.

We continued to haul and lose line back to the fish for almost another twenty minutes, but then it began to tire. Mike, hanging head down over the ship's side, shouted that our fish was big. Then he announced that we had a magnificent shark on the hook! After that we saw the fish regularly as it rose to the surface and began swimming around in circles that took it alternately into the light and then back under the boat into deep shadow. Luckily, to avoid ropes snagging around the propeller and rudder, all supply vessels have a metal skid that stops anything getting caught up. Gradually we retrieved nearly all of the line and could see our length of wire.

As Mike and the seaman pulled hard against the fish, I had the first go at tailing the shark. Making a noose around the handline, I shook it down to get it round the shark's head. The first time the fish tore through the loop, giving both lads burned fingers and a few heart-stopping moments, but on the second try the loop stayed around the shark's middle and I snatched it tight as it slid to the wrist of the tail. Three of us pulling on the rope and we had a subdued shark against the hull. The next problem was how to get the fish over the gunwale.

This was basic seamanship for our crewman, who made for the upper bridge deck. He swung out a davit and called for the end of the rope. Reaved through the pulley, we had enough purchase on the rope to lift the heavy fish easily. With a swish, it sailed across the rail and thumped on to the deck.

Mike Shepley with the only garfish left after our sharking episode!
At this size they could be regarded as a true oceanic gamefish species,
possessing incredible strength and speed.

Although I still cannot identify the species with certainty, my reference books on Indian ocean fish suggest it may have been an Indian ocean bull shark *Carcharhinus gangeticus*, although in colour and general shape it looked remarkably like the lemon shark of that area *Negaprion acutidens*. In any event, we had the fun and Mike kept the complete jawbones. The crew, having tumbled out of their bunks to see the monster, got the flesh to eat and the fins to sell in the Dubai Creek Market.*

There were a lot of 'guesstimates' about the shark's weight. Our skipper, to whom everyone deferred, shouted emphatically that it weighed 150 kilos (330 lbs) which looked about right – not at all bad for a handline!

We didn't get another shark, but spent our time fishing for remora, the fish that attach themselves to sharks and live in symbiotic association with the larger predator. It may be that those we hooked and boated had abandoned our shark when it was being fought on the line; anyway, there they were and eager to grab a slice of garfish.

---

* The discovery of such huge potential man-eaters must have come as a shock to the crews of the supply vessels. These capable seamen often spend their waiting hours at anchor diving below the hull to scrape off weed and shellfish that tend to reduce the boat's speed and efficiency!

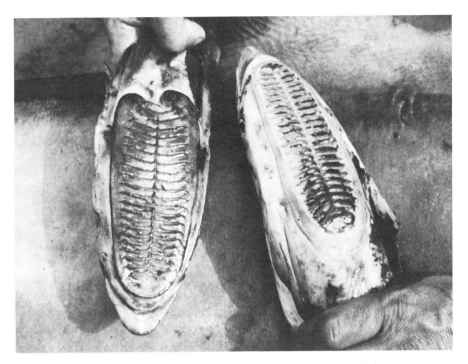

Remora have a sucker pad, on the top of their heads, with which they attach themselves to the host fish. In some ways the pad resembles the sole of a rubber boot!

The oilmen and sportfishers to whom we spoke later ashore, slightly spoiled the episode by assuring us that our particular shark wasn't big by Gulf standards! In fact, they had regularly seen hammerheads of over 11 feet long swimming around the oil and gas rigs. Fish that stay at the surface long enough to allow clear sightings of their species and length – now there's a temptation. If I'm spared, I just might save the pennies for a return trip!

CHAPTER TWENTY TWO

The Hybrids of Derryvony

IRELAND

Have you noticed how popular the hybrid has become over the years? Until recent times there was little written about these fish in the angling journals. Few anglers had caught a hybrid or, at any rate, correctly identified one among the contents of their keepnet. Then the bubble burst and suddenly everybody was talking about this freshwater phenomenon. The message to the angling world was clear. There was nothing new about these fish; they had always been around, unrecognized by all but the scientifically trained.

Although I knew that hybrids existed among members of the carp family, my first direct experience of them came when I caught what I imagined to be magnificent rudd from the River Shannon. All of them had huge golden scales

A perfect fish. I believe that it was a specimen rudd/bream hybrid, yet there were spawning tubercles on its head. Could this infer the ability to breed?

that appeared completely rudd-like but there was something odd about them. The fins had softer, muted colours, yet were enormous, out of proportion to the rest of the body. What really settled the 'difference' for me was the fight they put up. The fish fought like demons, displaying a battle that, for their body size, far exceeded anything that I had formerly experienced from the species. A close inspection gave the clue to their real origin. Each fish had a pronounced 'breamy' hump, that camel-like curve to the dorsal ridge which implies that a bream must be one of the parent fish.

No fully fledged rudd or bream had ever shown the fighting qualities displayed by these fish. From those far-off days on the Shannon I have enjoyed fishing for hybrids in a wide range of situations, from deep Irish loughs to Continental canals and rivers.

In 1983 I was introduced to some fishing that would make any angler sit up and beg. Francis McGoldrick, who keeps his family's pub, 'The Angler's Rest', in Ballyconnell's Main Street, offered to lead me, along with two companions, to a lake connected to the Woodford and Erne river systems. Francis insisted that it contained the best hybrid fishing that he'd found.

We had an initial problem finding the water. Take a look at a map of County Cavan and you will be flummoxed by the wealth of lakes and rivers that separate the patches of land. We began our search in the heart of the county, from Belturbet. We left the town and took a cross-country jaunt along the tiniest of leafy lanes. Passing waters that drew concerted gasps, Francis just shook his head and muttered, 'Not here, we're heading for big-fish country!'

On this introductory evening there was to be no fishing, only a flying visit to get the swims fed. Fred Tamplin, who in his non-fishing time makes a living as a groundbait manufacturer, had provided a sack of feed and some additives to get the chosen swims alive for the following day.

We hadn't counted on having to carry the sack of feed up one side of a steepish slope and down the other. Puffing harshly, for at that time each of us chose to disregard the Government warning on those packets, we topped the hill to find a vista of lakes and linking waterways that form the Upper Erne catchment area.

The lakes looked fishy and there wasn't a single house or human in sight. Freddie mixed the feed and we plonked it out in the water, along a 40-yard band at about four rod lengths from the clear, level shoreline. The plan was for all four of us to fish comfortably, side by side, along its length, with sufficient groundbait to pull and hold fish for the early morning session.

Retracing our ride through the Cavan lanes, we retired to well-earned pints at 'The Angler's Rest' to plan a campaign. A start was to be made, on the morrow, at around ten o'clock, after a massive breakfast to fortify us for a whole day's fishing. Francis, bless him, stole a march on us by getting out to the fishing before nine. I know, from experience of leading groups of anglers, that he simply wanted to check that all was well!

Francis McGoldrick playing a hybrid at Derryvony. Hidden way in rolling countryside, the lake is connected to the Erne catchment and feeds Ulster's largest river.

When we finally arrived at the lake, plodding our weary way up and down the hill, Francis was wearing the grin of success; not a 'One a Chuck' type leer, just that lazy curl of the mouth that lets everyone know they are in with a chance.

Plumbing for depth, I found that it was very deep. Even close in there must have been over 12 feet of water. A gusty wind established that we had to fish on the tip. I had set my heart on fishing the float and hadn't brought a quivertip rod with me. Thwarted, I made up my 13-foot Alacrity to rely on detecting bites at the tip. As it turned out, I had no problem. In fact quivertips danced so much in the strong breeze that my stiffish top joint became a distinct advantage. There was no doubting the first bites; rod tips were whipped round against the pressure of a wind that tore over the lake.

It took us members of the 'late arrivals club' only a few minutes to get set up to fish. Francis shouted that he already had quite a few hybrids among his catch of skimmers and roach. John Woods pulled the keepnet to inspect the catch. The roach/bream hybrid was easily detected. Slightly yellowish on the scaling, the fins also looked yellow, although there was wide variation and some were orange. The fish were solid, deep in the body and all had the typical breamy hump.

There was further evidence that our overnight feeding had paid off as three or four pairs of great crested grebes dived constantly to bring small roach to the surface from the area beyond our feed. I always enjoy the presence of waterbirds while fishing. If they inhabit any lake, it is a safe bet that the water is fertile. Creatures of the countryside don't waste time on a barren swim.

For the first hour we gradually built up our individual catches. Fred and John caught more roach than anything else, whereas Francis and I had mostly bream and hybrids. I can't explain why as we all fished similar baits, cast to the same area. Perhaps our lavish overnight feeding had pulled a massive shoal of roach that had settled to feed at the centre of the area, the bream and hybrids lingering to feed around the fringe of the groundbait.

This feeding behaviour didn't last, for within another hour or so the hybrids hit the swim in style. I found myself grabbing the camera to picture three rods arcing in unison, each connected to a fish weighing 2 lbs or more. There were no first thumping bites, followed by the easy pull associated with playing small common bream. These hybrids fought like tigers!

Fred and John, who had elected to fish the middle swims, often found themselves badly tangled as their fish ran sideways, dragging swimfeeders as they went. It takes a powerful fish to tow a swimfeeder, while putting up a decent fight in water that has only a gentle flow.

Farmers will tell you about hybrid vigour, gained by selective breeding. In many large freshwaters, different species, breeding on a non-selective basis, produce progeny that outfight either of its parent fish! We find both rudd/bream and roach/bream hybrids in Irish lakes and rivers. The former seem to grow larger, but the roach/bream hybrid in residence at Derryvony proved the truth of the argument by giving the tackle a hard time.

Fish in Cavan lakes display so many different characteristics that some-times I have my doubts as to what they really are. The degree of hybridization would seem to vary from fish to fish. Some of the hybrids caught look like a bronze bream, with only a little rudd or roach colour and scaling. Others appear completely reversed, possessing the scales and shape of roach or rudd, with large breamy fins, of muted colouring, suggesting only a minute amount of bream parent stock in their make-up. Perhaps there is some researcher in the laboratories of the Central Fisheries Board who would be able to enlighten us on the subject.

Fishing through the day, we built catches of around 70 lbs a man. Though mixed in variety, hybrids made up the bulk of each catch. There hadn't been enough time for adequate preparation nor were we able to work up the swim potential. This lake, lying only half a mile south of the Ulster border, will one day produce an enormous catch, probably to an angler who has the time to feed a swim over a prolonged period. There are fish in abundance, but it takes a lot of groundbait to draw and hold the larger shoals.

I find the sheer size of the Erne River system disconcerting. There is so much water through which the big shoals of fish can roam, yet only the larger lakes can provide enough feed to hold them for any length of time. Each of the connected waters has the vital ingredients necessary for a huge catch; plenty of natural food, only the slowest current drifting through and, so important to the fisherman, a situation well off the beaten track! Most of the better lakes are beyond the navigable section, which means little interference from boats; in fact, we saw only a solitary pike angler afloat. They are not likely to be overfished from the banks as few anglers appear willing to stumble across the hills and treed slopes, loaded with tackle and groundbait, to track down the hybrid shoals.

Hybridization is a fascinating subject and hybrid fish may be far more widespread than we think. Some authorities believe that these fish are only found in waters where there is insufficient space for the various species to breed on a selective principle. Surely, this cannot be true of the enormous loughs of Ireland!

In their book, *Freshwater Fishing*, Fred Buller and Hugh Falkus state that first-generation hybrids are unable to breed. It appears that American and Canadian ichthyologists have done work which suggests that some hybrids (between various pike species), although unable to reproduce their own kind, can be crossed back to their original, pure, parent stock. Is it possible that cyprinoids have a similar facility? Either way, the presence of these interesting fish adds up to a great deal of confusion among anglers who find the 'odd' examples in their keepnets.

CHAPTER TWENTY THREE

Return To Kerry

IRELAND

There can be nothing worse for a bass angler than to arrive on a strand that is heaving with surf without a plentiful supply of good worms! It happened to me a year or so ago on the Ring of Kerry when I was paying a return visit to a beach that held fond memories.

I had been fishing on the Dingle Peninsula, knocking out dogfish from Ventry Bay and trying desperately to dig some useful bait from the beds at Clogharne. I didn't find many useful lugworm at all, just a few miniature lugs and some small ragworm that might have graced a hook intended for flatties, but certainly not as bass baits.

In the end I bought some frozen mackerel from the fish plant in Dingle town before driving round to the Ring. It's a second rate bait in my opinion, but better than nothing. Rienko Baarslag and I took off in the car, around the deeply-indented bay past Inch Strand to try our luck on the more southerly peninsula. We headed for Ballinskelligs Bay, intending to fish a quiet corner tucked below the Waterville Bay hotel. It had become a favourite shore mark of mine, producing many plump bass over the years. This was Rienko's first visit to Ireland, a vastly different landscape from his home in Holland.

We arrived to find a beautiful surf, a creaming, crashing line of power hatched in the middle of the Atlantic. We made an early start, on the young flood tide, reasoning that to get a bait into the water, even before the fish arrive, is better than smoking or indulging in some other time-wasting occupation.

The early flood brought us nothing, apart from the occasional knock from a healthy clump of free-swimming weed – the kind that always gets itself gathered at the leader knot! The problem with filamentous weed is that by gradually building up on the knots it masks the quiet pulls of a big bass. Consequently, I prefer to wind in and rebait when I detect weed on the nylon. This keeps a smellier, fresher bait in the water, rather than one with all traces of oil attraction washed out.

Ballinskelligs is not really an open bass strand. The inner bay is protected by a ring of rocky headlands and islands that tend to reduce the full force of any oceanic breaker rhythm. But when there is a touch of west in the wind, the surf takes on the regular pattern of a tremendous bass beach.

One off-putting feature, other than our rapidly-softening mackerel bait, arrived in the shape of a 50 plus-feet trawler that proceeded to drag up and down on the deepwater line, which is marked by the distinct colour change. The thought struck me that the combination of trawlers and nylon gill nets, remnants of which can be seen on almost any Irish bass beach, don't give bass fishers much of a chance these days. Fortunately, this was to be one occasion when the commercial fisherman didn't have the last laugh!

As the boat began its second haul around the bay, wheeling for position just outside the outer surf line, I had a magnificent knock. Classical it was – just as all the books predict! Rienko had a simultaneous bite, so we found ourselves

recovering line together. It wasn't really fair, because there I was attempting to get him his first Irish bass and when the lines were nearly in we saw our two fish clearly in the smooth table of water. Mine was a bass of about 4 lbs and his a flounder that had somehow lassoed itself in the trace. Nevertheless, they were proof that the Ballinskelligs shore mark still fished, despite the trawlers and commercial pressures from a host of EEC interests, and both taken on bait that shouldn't have attracted the lowliest of shore crabs!

The next morning I set out for some decent bait. Meeting a local farmer on the road, his load of freshly cut bog turf hauled by a wiry donkey, a few words about the day and mention of fishing elicited information that the tiny

Evening on the strand at Ballinskelligs Bay, Co. Kerry. There are many favoured hotspots along the bay – I prefer the headland below the hotel.

Late evening and the bass are beginning to feed in the breakers at
Ballinskelligs; another good fish followed by a wash and shave might
not come amiss!

harbour at Ballinskelligs was the place for lugworm. True enough, there on
the right-hand side of the quay wall was a patch of mud and sand, sprinkled
with small rocks and wrack, that had every sign of a worm bed. It was the
easiest digging that I had done in years. Great fleshy lugworm were only a spit
deep, often three or four coming up on the prongs of a fork in one lift; twenty
minutes provided enough worms for two men fishing a night tide.

We drove back to our strand to wait for the tide to build. Early flow saw the
arrival of a couple of English lads, who fished for an hour or so and then left. I
must admit that I, too, don't care much for the first hour of flood, preferring to
wait for the full force of mid-tidal strength to hit the sand. From then on, until
the turn to the ebb, seems to be the best of bass fishing. The departure of the
other anglers was typical of modern shore fishing, where men expect fish to
come almost immediately and if that doesn't happen off they go chasing fish
around the coast. Fish arrive in their own time and for their own reasons. If a
beach or rocky coast has food, they will turn up at some stage of a tide!

In the west of Ireland, even when a miles-long strand is deserted, a local
farmer will inevitably be watching your efforts from some vantage point or
other. Staring out to sea, I heard the soft footfalls that heralded the arrival of
somebody behind me. The old fellow had come along the golden strand, after

inspecting my small touring caravan, and began giving freely of his knowledge. He had always found the best of bass fishing to come in the small dark
hours (twilight) when the fish didn't see too well, confirming my observation
that fish always appeared to concentrate tight up to the rocky headland that
ends the strand below the hotel. 'Fish against the rocks, into the black water,'
were his parting words. We rebaited our hooks and cast as close to the
darkening rocks as was prudent.

Within ten minutes I had an offer that nearly grabbed the rod from my
hands, indicating the arrival of bass. Unfortunately, because of the sudden-
ness of the take, I missed it. In panic, I walloped the rod back in a massive
strike, failing to take up slack line between me and the fish. The lesson is to
take at least two strides back to pick up slack line that nearly always develops
when there is a surf running. My fish had moved in toward me after lifting the
bait. I ought to have used a grip lead, which would have prevented the
problem, as its buried grip wires pull the fish up sharply, hooking it when it
moves off. Instead, I had chosen to equip the terminal rig with a plain torpedo
weight that could roll the bait around in the moving water!

As it happened, the next bite was more certain. This fish tore offshore
toward the deep water. A gentle, almost lazy, sweep of the rod gave me
instant contact, with the thumping message that I had a hooked bass on my
line. I'd kept the plain bomb lead on so the fish was better able to show how it
could fight in the tumbling surf. Aware of the proximity of the rocks, the bass
gave an unexpected sideways dash, turning again and again, but gradually
quietened to run in on the tables of water that eased toward my waders.

Later, Rienko asked me to look after his rod while he ran off to make a cup of
coffee, and a bite came within seconds – a textbook 'snatch' from a 'schoolie',
quick and rattling, that set the rod dancing in his rest. I made a frantic grab,
still holding my own rod, struck, thought I had contact for a second or so and
then knew that I had lost somebody a first bass. Ah, well, that's fishing. . . .

By the time we hit our beds for the night the tally was two bass landed, with
at least ten hard bites from others that somehow didn't get hooked.

Next morning I had the fruits of sustained effort. In the hammering surf *and*
under the blazing sun of a fine Kerry day, a bass of nearly 5 lbs hit my bait
hard, ran seaward and gave me the fight that I had travelled all this way for. I
had persisted with a free-running leger and no griplead, and the result was
the sort of battle bass fishing is all about, in which a fine fish is allowed,
unhindered, to prove its ability.

*   *   *   *   *

Most sea anglers today would agree that bass fishing isn't what it was. Yet
although there can be no more massive catches, at least the bass seems to be a
surviving species, still capable of pulling anglers on to the lonely strands of

our western shores. What is vital, however, is to reduce the number of gillnets that are spread about without regard to the damage they do. Although owners claim that the nets are set to catch salmon and seatrout, they take a terrible toll of bass and other inshore species that haunt the tideline. Considering the time it takes for a bass to reach any appreciable size, the species is particularly vulnerable to the predation imposed upon it. In sporting terms, its value, both to anglers and rod-carrying tourists, remains paramount.

*   *   *   *   *

Looking back over my fishing, I may have tasted the vintage years; when bass fishing was frantic, when a fresh-run salmon and I could arrive simultaneously at a pool or when huge, hardly imaginable pike smashed through the reeds ahead of my dinghy – those were generous times.

In the future, as age slows me to a more sedate pace, there will be a need to plan my safaris more carefully; perhaps taking time to write ahead to local anglers before piling all the gear into the car. There is definitely a case for re-appraising the fishing that lies virtually in my own backyard. I know that for years I have passed it by in favour of hearsay about 'legendary monsters' purported to swim in waters over the horizon.

Whatever happens, I will continue to fish – for this sport has given me many friends and I admit to still being well and truly hooked. . . .